BURNERS & BLACK MARKETS

LANCE HENDERSON

COPYRIGHT

Copyright 2016 Lance Henderson
All Rights Reserved.

PREFACE

Hell hath no fury like a woman scorned.

Scorned might be the wrong word choice here, since it was I who invited the Homeland Security agents into my house.

"Come on in, the water's warm," I told them.

They walked in like vampires. It felt queasy to walk behind them, like today was some kind of an initiation day or something. One of them (the female) hummed softly as she came in. Some death row harmonica tune as I recall, probably from Shawshank Redemption.

To be honest neither resembled Mulder or Scully like I thought they would (nor had a gun that I could see), but they were dressed for the job. Both agents sounded professional: suited up and as stone-faced as any statue on Easter Isle with little in the way of humor or human warmth. In fact the male agent looked every bit the consummate professional hitman Alberto the Shadow was in Scarface. You didn't turn your back on a guy like that.

Yet here I was contemplating asking them to leave after only inviting them in a nanosecond ago. Wasn't happening. Worse was the whiff of air my nostrils caught scent of as they passed. It was the scent of something dead. Or maybe just the last guy that asked them to leave prematurely.

As I poured out a drink I asked myself: Were they really agents? I couldn't tell. I suppose I should have asked for ID but I was still feeling jet-lagged from the Rio trip. With two days to go before Mardi Gras, I'd raced home from the New Orleans airport to get some sleep so I could meet my brother to fast-paint an Endymion parade float at mom's house. Only this time I'd be late. Terribly late.

A fitting end I suppose, since my brother Stephen and I have PhDs in lateness. Like clockwork I had waited until the 11th hour to do what Mom tasked us with: paint the Endymion float fast and neat and all cool like something out of Willy Wonka. Only fast and *neat* where we were concerned was like asking the Marx brothers to do a rush job on a Mona Lisa forgery. I could paint well enough, but my brother, like Groucho, painted single-handedly with one hand holding a joint as the other brushed. Hustling was his specialty, not painting. He hustled everything. Even me.

He'd often give me a list of places where his friends lay in wait along Veterans Blvd near New Orleans, friends who dressed the part but none of whom were actually veterans. The mission? Bomb them with the best booty and beads when our float came around. Only knowing my brother like I do, he'd brag down at Igor's bar long and loud like some train in the night and take all the credit. I'd get nothing.

The man never gave credit for squat unless he was in trouble with the law. Even as far back as sixth grade, he'd scoff whenever I said to knock off the bar bragging in the school yard. It never helped. Sooner or later, I warned, a shark would come along and sink a mouthful of teeth into those lying teeth of his.

Then one scorcher of a day in August (middle school, as I recall), a thresher shark showed up when he caught the attention of the local police. It seemed one freckled boy told every other boy in the school yard that my brother had bragged he owned a shed containing every automatic weapon imaginable, even (I kid you not) a suitcase nuke straight out of Fallout. They all bought this lie, of course, only one of the ugly kids he'd teased had ratted him out. Shocker, right? Next thing you know our puritan principal summoned him and the cops and when the boys in blue arrived, they cuffed him like he'd pinched every girl's bum in the yard.

I sat there mumbling and trembling in Ms. Needles math class like I was next on the hit list. Had I overheard the words 'search warrant'? And that odd scent that one of the cops dragged with her. Perfume? It reeked of dead shark.

Truth be told I was more worried about the secret stash. They'd steal my porn stash and take Suzanne Somers away from me forever, I was sure of it. Asses would sting (yours truly) and if not by Dad than surely that sharkey cop with the razor-thin mustache whose last name sounded an awful lot like 'thresher'.

But my brother didn't rat. They suspended him and Dad hit the roof, but he didn't rat. Turned out that my father pulled some strings to keep him out of jail. The lucky loser.

Fast forward to now, in my living room, and that same shark cop from sixth grade eying me in perfect dark; eyes filled with wet Texas crude. She'd no doubt had eaten a few dinosaurs by now, slit a few throats on the way to the top, and now here she was staring me down like I was a fresh-born kitten meant for the grill. Come on in, the water's warm, I'd said.

My brother was in trouble again. A deep sea of trouble.

It seemed that he had targeted hidden Tor sites scattered around the Darknet, playing his usual lame pranks, when in one instance he took it too far. The two agents came because, well, Stephen just didn't know when to leave on a high note. He had told two undercover agents that he owned an underground storage bunker full of illegals that he sold off as sex slaves for a grand a pop. A side hustle, he called it. I knew this to be a prank, but they did not. How could they?

Only now the very shark I'd warned him about had come back to bite *me*. Oh irony. Teaching Tor when he didn't understand the risks posed by Google and all other social media tyrants was a colossal blunder of biblical proportions on my part. A terrible mistake and one I'd not likely recover from. It was like handing Frodo's Ring of Power to one of those guys down at the Bayou Swamp Tour that stick their heads into the mouths of crocs for a few dollars more. A lot of fat good it'd do.

Oh and he had used a cell phone. Brilliant, right?

It hadn't been hard to track the goober down. Google had helped them connect-the-dots. Now they were here for a side of beef off my backside, the only question being which side.

So I escorted the agents into my kitchen expecting to be butchered by my own knives. I politely I offered them a beer or a Coke or a steak. Hell even a three month old Twinkie, which they declined. I huffed and then straddled a bar stool and invited them to do the same. Once again they declined. They could not be bought, bribed or bamboozled for any price.

"This won't take long," the male agent said. It's what all agents said, everywhere. Even the census taker has said the same a year prior and as I recall it'd taken forever and a day. The next words he said cut like dry ice.

"We take every threat to this nation seriously, Lance. Your brother has made some serious threats," said the taller agent as he crossed his bulky arms. "He's in our custody now but whether he stays there depends on you. In this very instant."

Custody? I didn't believe him. "Do tell," I said as I folded my skinny arms.

"We'd like to see your phone."

My heart stopped as all color drained from my face, all monochrome.

"Ahem. Right now," added the female agent. It was then that I asked for ID. They showed it but it was too late. They were in like Flynn.

"Prostitution rings carry a hefty sentence as does issuing threats to federal law enforcement officers," the agent began to say, "... and even dumping manure on our department's front lawn."

He glanced around the kitchen, running his hand along the granite countertop.
    "Asset forfeiture is a big industry these days." He knocked on granite.

No shit, I thought. Asset forfeiture, courtesy of the ATF and DEA, had been a very profitable industry for eons and all the more for the US government. I'd known guys with small basement grow-ops that lost their homes and land to the Feds both in Canada and the States. I took nothing for granted where those guys were concerned.

But I knew not to talk without a lawyer present... except I'd already invited them in and like true vampires it became apparent that they weren't keen on leaving without the item they came for. Why oh why me. With my voice quaking I let out a little protest that ended up sounding more like a mew instead of a roar. A cat going to the vet.

"I'm not giving you my phone," I squeaked. "I don't care what kooky story my idiot brother told you."

"Excuse me?" the lady asked. She giggled at this, a giggle that sounded like a cat chewing up a squishy mouse or toothpaste squeezed out of a tube. "You cannot win against the federal government. Hand it over."

"Hand what over?"

"THE PHONE."

" Oh, that. Err... No."

"No? Why not?" the thresher chick asked.

I stabbed a finger at her as I raised my voice. "Either make an arrest or leave! I'll not be bullied into submission without a warrant by a couple of federal thugs named Frick and Frack. My phone is encrypted so it'll do you no good anyway. But I've got a landline here and my lawyer on retainer so let me just call him up and get a recording going."

They both looked at each other. "We'll be back," the man said. As they closed the door I heard the lock slide into place like a jail cell slamming home. My cell phone was about to become my jail cell. Had I hammered the last nail into my own coffin?

Furiously I sped over to my brother's house, so fast I nearly hit a dog peeing on a fire hydrant and didn't stop to look back. I was livid. *Beyond* livid. I had no clue if Agent Frick would be back, warrant in one hand and a noose in the other, but I'd be damned if I was going to swing from the nearest tree without knowing what stupid thing my brother'd done to bring on this level of heat.

I found him parked outside his spooky old house in that fire-engine red truck I'd hated for years, AC-DC blaring Back in Black. He was twirling his pornstache, no worry in the world about his fate or mine. Typical. I wanted to smack him. Hard. Right upside his head the way Rick James did to a few tag-a-longs back in the 80s. But I stopped when I saw Facebook front and center. Not only *that* abomination but Twitter, Google Plus, Skype, Viber and Whatsapp, with Tor running in the background.

Tor! Sweet lawd almighty.

I grit my teeth and shouted "DUMMY!" into his ear and watched as his phone fell into his Bud Light glass under the hot pink fuzzy dice. He cursed me out brothers only can.

"Azzzzhole," he yelled. He wiped it off, waterproof. Gangly and unshaven, he resembled the skinny gyro captain from Road Warrior who believed in the concept of shared wealth - as long as it belonged to someone else.

"Couple of goons hassled me today," he mumbled. "Same here... *brother*." I replied. "Somethin' about you making threats? And... a manure dump on a federal building's front lawn?"

After a long sigh, a belch and a few coarse threats I finally dragged the intel out of him. How he'd not only issued threats over Tor but that he'd put in an order for a dump truck to pile a ton of manure on the FBI and Homeland Security's front lawn using a credit card over Tor. *My* credit card. He pulled it from his wallet and frisbeed it into my face with the stupidest comment I'd ever heard.

"Tor didn't work with your card. You ain't paid up or somethin'?"

It was here that I went dark on him.

I pulled the knuckle-dragger out and inside the house kicking and screaming before letting loose with every curse I knew. He flailed like the swordfish we caught in the Gulf of Mexico, fins everywhere like a crazy person, swinging and sweating and stabbing.

When we finally simmered down I noticed the state of his living room. The place was ransacked more than usual. Beer cans piled high with a vacant space where the PC had been lie visible. Three guesses as to who took it. The FBI had come and let it slide but apparently they had friends in Homeland who needed a fresh piece of meat. Two slabs actually, order up.

When I pressed him on it he replied that Homeland carted it away while powered on using a portable power source. I knew about such things, but did he? Nope.

He tried to get up so I shoved him back down and yelled, "You stay in that spot and don't you move a muscle until I'm finished!"

I threw everything I'd said the week prior into his face again (opsec stuff mostly), and swore I'd take mom's house back in a New York minute if he didn't listen this time. It wasn't enough that his ass and ego stung. He needed a lobotomy.

"You're good at that nekkid Tor stuff. I ain't! 'Sides, you talk too fast how in hell can I keep up with that technical mojo?"

He was right. I always talked too fast even back in sixth grade and on a few sweaty occasions I could swear that I could literally see my words flying over and around his uncombed head; like if you shined a flashlight through those ears you'd see his eyes flash. So I went slow. Turtle slow. Talking with my hands like some Italian piano player before a grand performance.

"Look," I began. "If you're going to play the Riddler and prank alphabet agencies then the absolute least you can do is to muck it all up in your own name and do so with some residue of competence. It's embarrassing when my name comes into it. Why'd you use my card for it? Why bring me into it at all?"

Nothing but deadbeat excuses came back.

My voice went as low and deadly serious as a neurosurgeon when discussing a terminal patient. I wanted to take a red hot searing iron of opsec rules to his butt cheeks but knowing him he'd forget they were there. So instead I decided what he needed was a foundation of the basics, the why, the wherewithal, the way, the whole enchilada when it came to cell phones and anonymity. Why we do *this* instead of *that* and what happens if we *don't*.

"Why?" he'd ask.

"Because guys who never sweat the small stuff as long as the power button is greenlit get burned, that's why."

Then along comes some taffer with a badge and a gruff voice who hits him with one small threat and then another and another, and all in a friendly 'knock and talk' and at that point he might as well slap the cuffs on himself. He doesn't see the overall context, the trap being set, and ends up like Gulliver with the Lilliputians, pinned to the ground by a million tiny threads he can't even see.

I talked about the giants: Google. Twitter. Facebook. How the lying scumbags were little more than modern-day witch hunters who cooperated with cops to enforce a gazillion laws no one cared about but made them millions every year.

I droned on about encryption, explaining how it always worked it's wonders if it was automatic and running under the hood. I told him he had lazy man's opsec, a clown's, and that sooner or later someone would throw a grenade into that clown's wardrobe and it'd make all the papers with nice colorful photos of his private stash all laid bare. I told him of the types of encryption most used, HTTPS in the browser and cell to tower connections for his cellular calls, that they performed so well because he was *unaware of their presence.*

"Encrypt everything," I repeated. I hammered this over and over, especially on cell phones no matter if he had something to hide or not. "It should be there and working its magic under the hood without you having to hit the ON switch."

"Why?" he asked.

"Because if you're only going to flip that encryption switch when and only when you need to secure your data, you relay that data's significance as though you'd pulled a fire alarm."

We talked about Tor and it's brother Freenet and how both are used by Chinese dissidents but that since *every* Chinese dissident uses those apps that this has caused problems for anyone wanting real anonymity. If its only used for committing dissident-like things then China's ruling elite class can cherry-pick anyone off one by one and all by that one lone homing signal. The same that the FBI had done (with a little help from my credit card).

Then I said that the reverse is equally true.

"If everybody employs encryption *everywhere*, then instead of it being a signal to the fire department to come put out a fire, it becomes impossible to tell who is using it to chat about Leonardo DeCaprio's latest round of clubgirls from someone intent on sparking a revolution. Use encryption for every little thing you do and you'll save lives on the other side of the planet without even knowing it."

He shot me a dumbfounded look like encryption had nothing to do with cell phones or Tor.

"If you'd bothered to pay attention in sixth grade, you'd have learned all about state-sanctioned liars like the Gestapo in Nazi Germany and KGB in Soviet Russia, enough to see through that agent's lies." I pointed to the door. "Like Agent Frick. Didn't her name seem familiar to you?"

"You shut your mouth!" he snapped. "They had a no-knock warrant what was I supposed to do, tell em' to get lost?"

"You just answered your own question."

"Huh?"

"You shut your mouth. You said it brother. You don't say squat without an attorney."

He thought on this for a long while before I continued.

"Something else, too. You also failed on account of having an unencrypted phone and PC. If the encrypted data is in *your* hands and not *theirs* you're in less danger of being bullied around. You have more leeway. Do China dissidents? In China once they *take away* encryption and guns, they'll seize your property rights, birth rights, your progeny and what follows after that is a bloody mutiny or complete slavery where all legal rights are changed so that you cannot resist. You cannot fight back."

"And after that?" he asked.

"Who knows. The Stalinist regime may enact a murder campaign to eliminate anyone perceived as an enemy of the state. That's anyone with a gun or encrypted files. You saw what happened to all those screaming Muslims over there in Beijing a few years back. They rounded up all those fools and shot them at dawn and didn't look back."

"Probably didn't wait till dawn I reckon," he said. "They ain't used encryption though is what I heard."

I smiled. "Might not have helped anyway. But thank God for the 5th amendment in the United States."

A long silence. I needed one more example. Something modern.

"Look at Apple and the FBI. The Feds wanted to set a precedent in breaking that terrorist's phone."

"Precedent? Why's that?" he asked.

"Take any random shooter's phone. The FBI already has the chat logs, flash drives, and iCloud data from them. They just make those statements to get public support for backdoors since there's nothing the data on the iPhone can tell them that they don't know already."

"But if that happens..."

"Everyone's screwed a hundred ways from Sunday. Apple gave the them access to everything that exists and still gave them additional forensic advice on top of that. That fact alone proved it was a backdoor fishing expedition."

"Yeah. Yeah yer right I figger."

"And it's impossible for a backdoor to target just one phone. Any new backdoor will target everyone's phone, every class, at a minimum, such as one iPhone 5c affecting all the others. The FBI wants Apple to code in a backdoor that's signed by Apple without messing up the decryption keys. Do that and it would almost certainly escalate international tensions about European privacy too, not just the US."

He nodded slowly.

"They'd blot out any hope of Safe Harbor for good by proving that safe harbor is anything but 'safe'."

Underneath his long-sleeved shirt I could see he was wearing a that hideous Lord of the Rings tee, still grey and ragged and reeking of the same cheap Bud Light Lime he'd swigged on opening night. At the tip I could see it was either Gandalf or Saruman peeking over the mountaintops. I couldn't tell which.

"This isn't Saruman tinkering around. This is global Sauron, creating his Ring."

"But I'm just *one* guy. *One* peon."

"You only need *one* guy, *one* peon."

I pointed out the window, up at the clouds. "See that? Picture yourself way up there in a grand hall with your great-grandfather and several generations of your lineage going back eons when they're all telling their brave tales. Imagine telling them with a straight face that you left it up to some other peon because you weren't up to learning how to evade not only Google but the NSA and the FBI because it's easier to just focus on you and your late nights blowing money on anti-freeze daiquiris and Angry Birds or Facebook updates and pranking the FBI building with a truckload of bullshit."

"Now imagine them shaking their heads in disgust at this overgrown kid too proud to build out a fortress of doom - a guy whose only concerns were for his own hide and to hell with what his forefathers fought for. They'd view you as lacking courage and any sense of ethics. They'd look upon you as a lesser human being. A joke to humanity. A sheep. Can you imagine Frodo doing that to Elrond, Gandalf, Legolas and the rest of the crew and giving them a three-fingered salute as he slid that ring down his finger and snuck off into the night?

"Hale no."

"Me neither. When push comes to shove it's our *nonactions* and not our actions that bury us. We dig our own graves far too often enough, brother, so let's not pay others to do it while we're still breathing. In the meantime I'll show you how to smooth that ring down your finger so you can give whoever *else* wants to spy on you a nice three-fingered salute."

I looked over and noticed a few synapses misfiring. But a little confusion wasn't the end of the world. So I showed him something from his favorite social media outlet. Youtube. The very same he'd used with Tor, something even he could see the wisdom of employing. It was a classroom lecture called 'Don't Talk to Cops'. Nothing to do with cell phones, mind you, but everything to do (or not to do) when a couple of G-Men show up at your house making unruly demands.

The day after that, I beat him to death with every opsec trick I knew on how to truly be anonymous on a smartphone, be it Android, Blackberry, iPhone... anywhere, at any time.

And what I showed him that day is what I'm about to show you. Right now.

CELL OPSEC AND THE POWERS THAT BE

"No one cared who I was until I put on the mask."
- *Bane, The Dark Knight Rises*

Why The Government Hates Anonymity

Most governments hate anonymity. They hate encryption too, but mostly anonymity since it covers a much broader range of the mutiny they fear. Every time someone learns how to communicate *anonymously*, that iron death-grip that they hold on a person's life loosens like you wouldn't believe. The media paints it a different color, of course. They say that it's *anonymity* that drives all the internet's ills.

. . .

You've heard it all before. Sexual harassment. Bullying. Date rape. Hackers. Identity thieves. Flying purple monkeys. And that if only we give the powers that be more reach or a longer vine into our private lives, then every bully and ogre'll burst into pillars of salt (instantly!) while the world trips right into a land of rainbows, unicorns and yellow submarines with a lofty lolling Ringo Starr leading the charge.

You already know it to be fake, of course. As fake as Data's artificial thumb.

But, I'll let you in on a secret not many know. And that is this. Anonymity encourages objectivity. Seriously, it does. It forces you to judge a person by the merits of their words alone.

Think about it. How many times have you heard an interview of some new jazz artist or guitarist whose Randy Rhoads-like riffs made your hour long commute more bearable, but somehow lacked that one ingredient that'd make them perfect in your mind's eye? You find yourself never fully satisfied with what you know of him, so you dig deeper. And deeper.

IT'S ABOUT CONTROL

You want to know every dirty little detail of his life, then weigh those details against his opinion. Little details like

- His politics.
- His religion.
- His favorite foods.
- Which websites he likes and which he hates.

What movies he watches. What car he drives. What sexual preference he likes. You could go on forever nitpicking the poor guy.

And it's dirty ethics to judge a person's merit in this way. But that's the way the global elite do it, every day, every hour. They prefer you make snap judgments because it reveals a ton of things about you as well. Things that are all easily trackable.

Let's face it. It's so much easier to blow someone's idea off if they happen to be favoring the other guy running for President rather than judge a person by what is said. So they focus on the man's upbringing. Or race. Or gender. Or which side their ancestors fought on during the Civil War. You can get to a point where you run out of ad hominem's to hurl.

IT'S ABOUT POWER

Dangerous ideas are good for anonymity. Try saying something outrageous on a political forum during an election year, but under a pseudonym. Use a cell phone without the aid of Tor. Note the hesitation you feel when you think of writing under your real name and saying something only someone like Smaug from the Hobbit would have the red-hot balls to say. That's the power I'm talking about. Anonymity grants that to you. It allows you to share controversial thoughts without fear of your house being firebombed with Molotov cocktails filled with flaming manure. And there's a few more perks I'll add to the bonfire.

- Anonymity prevents you from getting fired for disagreeing.
- It prevents Google from getting your private data and selling it.
- It prevents you from being the target of stalkers, hitmen, and even an angry former lover intent on showing the world the raging alcoholic she lived with some 17 years ago - never mind that you've

given up booze for ten years straight, all because she doesn't like the guy you're campaigning for (yes, yours truly).

The reason why people are opposed to anonymity is that they want to bully, harass and oppress people they disagree with. It's because it's always easier to discredit the man than his ideas. When you get right down to it, <u>total</u> 100% honesty can only be accomplished anonymously.

"Well," you start to say. "You don't need security if you aren't doing something illegal."

But that's how they want you to think.

It's like saying you may as well not lock your door unless you're a thief. Same thing. We all have to take action to protect our families and assets from those who steal, harm or burn. It's risk versus payoff, and where your freedom and peace of mind is concerned, the payoff is *always* worth it.

Imagine that you live in the Ninth Ward in New Orleans, hurricane season. A city with thousands of law abiding citizens (and maybe 10,000 criminals). You install a good lock on your front door because it's wise to do so. Likewise, you should install one on whatever portal you use to connect to the Internet. In most people's case, this means their cell phone.

That brings up the dirty word called encryption. That is, encrypting your connection. All connections, but cell phones especially. Most people shy away from this because they think they need to be some kind of superhacker or that real hackers only target celebrities like Jennifer Lawrence.

For example, if Facebook forgets to encrypt your data, any governmental agency can use this data to corral dissidents like you and I and those who'd make bitter enemies in the event of a revolution - all into a nice little easy-to-read Matrix-green display for a round-up when the proverbial crap hits the fan. This isn't all. Questions like "Who was your best friend in high school?" can lead to other accounts being compromised.

It's the same whenever I have to shred sensitive documents. Taxes, transcripts, copies of old love letters, copies of passports. I can say 'screw it' and shred only a few things since I hate sorting them all. But all it takes for my security model to collapse is one broken link in the chain. Much less headaches to shred EVERY sensitive document and gain peace of mind over having to sort each and every one of them.

Therefore it's best to learn how to encrypt <u>everything</u> from the beginning instead of trying to cherry pick which is the 'best' document to be encrypted. You avoid not only government agencies like the IRS and DEA but also stalkers, vindictive ex-spouses and former business partners. It's much easier to lose a fully encrypted device than one with only a few encrypted folders. Encryption is not just about preventing eavesdroppers from reading data. It also prevents them from changing it.

ANONYMITY AND PRIVACY

<u>Anonymity:</u>

Noun an·o·nym·i·ty \,a-nə-ˈni-mə-tē\: the quality or state of being unknown to most people : the quality or state of being anonymous.

Good ol' Webster, who never fails to give us a watered down definition on how to not do something of paramount importance. The word itself comes from Greek and means 'without a name', but that doesn't really tell us how to be invisible. Two points to make on this.

First, if we're talking about *true anonymity*, the kind where you're really off the grid and can stay off the radar even if a Delta Force team is sent in to capture you, then you're not only nameless but *traceless*. This book will be of little use to you because you're a Houdini already and Houdinis rarely like to have helpers. They prefer going it alone. It's the same if you're a famous old timer with old money, celebrity status or fame who can buy your way out of the country without a passport.

But traceless anonymity - which many believe an impossibility on cell phones - gets harder to maintain just as a boat's navigation wheel becomes harder to control in a thunderstorm. One jab in the right place will sink a boat just as surely as if Zeus himself lit one up in her backside and it won't matter how much you spent on polishing her tushy. The same happened to me when Hurricane Katrina slammed home in 2005.

KATRINA

A Category-5 hurricane, also known as the 'finger of God', came pretty close to sending me and my frizzy cat up to the pearly gates on a lightning bolt.

The wind barely took off a few shingles at first. No big deal I thought. It happens in most heavy storms after all. Then the kitchen window shattered. Then another. And another. Then the darkness came, only before I could panic I heard a propane tank blow up in the garage.

BOOM.

I know what you're thinking. Propane tanks don't just explode or implode or rupture or come apart on their own. In fact, an exploding propane tank is a rarity and doesn't happen nearly as often as the zombie movies portray. Only this one did because in a Cat-5 hurricane, anything's possible.

Truth be told, I didn't care about the tank. I was more worried about the darkness. That darkness was so thick you could feel it crawl onto your skin like some tar-covered gelatinous monster straight out of The Thing. I looked out onto the street and I remember thinking a lot of fat good anonymity did in this situation. I couldn't see or hear squat but I could worry. Oh yes, on that I was an ace, the top of the class. No question.

I tried to calm myself but it only got worse as I couldn't remember where I'd put the candles the last time this happened. I did know broken windows were replaceable though. They were, right? Yes, of course. Besides, how many times had the electricity gone out when it rained? Every afternoon if you lived in New Orleans and it seemed to happen all the time no matter Mardi Gras or Jazzfest or how many crocs swam down the street when the sewers clogged up. You could set your watch by it.

Soon I had two feet of water in my living room and Fritz the cat was looking pretty pathetic, like a wet hamster who'd stuck it's paw into an electrical socket. Panicked, the meows began to sound like those wailing police sirens on CSI. I couldn't understand a thing and to be honest he sounded a lot like Charlie Brown's teacher after a smoke and a stroke. He wanted out as did I.

I looked out to see the marina sailboats bobbing like bathtub ducks when the howling wind began to whistle and whirl through every room in the house, with a couple of my favorite anonymity books floating out the front door. Bad luck or poetic justice?

"Screw these shenanigans!" I said. Who'd ever gamble that this storm was the whisk-you-off-to-Oz variety? Not me. And not the cat as far as I could tell. Only a moment later, it got worse. A lot worse.

The storm began to blow in a lot of small objects from the street up and over the gutter. Pine cones. Coke cans. A Mardi Gras necklace that'd been stuck on the telephone wire for ages. Stripper panties. A nuke-green Hand Grenade drink container from Tropical Isle, New Orleans most powerful drink which admittedly was pretty tasty though it looked like an alien sex toy. At any rate I was in for some serious wind-based PTSD.

And with so many holes in my home, something struck me. I realized that any passerby could see inside and get a glimpse of my goods. All of em. I was unarmed and, God help me, without a Rottweiler to fend off any looters. Dead man walking. The looters I'd scared off during the previous flood might return for seconds if the storm got bad enough, and this time I was sure it would. Fritz and I were sitting ducks so I grabbed him in all his wet tuxedo fur and jumped into my fire-engine-red truck and headed off to the Northshore an hour away. The cat was now down to 3 lives.

First Point:

The first point is that one weak point can kill any security perimeter you thought you'd set up just as surely as my own broken windows killed mine. Maybe it was bad electrical lines. Loose ones. One lightning strike ended it. Boom and done.

With only one window gone a vagrant (or varmint or mutant) might've peeked inside for shelter and quickly deduced from the street garbage that it was an abandoned house. With every window gone, that same bum doesn't have to peek inside. He can see from the street what I've got. No guns? No dogs? Nothing? Oh but he sees the display case with a lot of shiny objects inside that he can pawn.

Why, even a brass lantern that'd fetch a few coins. Later I'd return to see a floating corpse, one straight out of The Walking Dead, floating near my house. I never quite recovered from that grisly sight.

In any case, I knew I couldn't sleep there since it'd be like using multiple layers of condoms given by an ex-stalker.

Each one with small holes. What did help me was having walkie-talkies at my disposal. Not Tor.

And not Skype or Google Chat or any other corporate solution, where the entirety of my conversations gets sold on a silver platter to the highest bidder. Those guys have only their own interests in mind, none of which involve my safety. They care up to the point when they can make truckloads of cash. That and the act of filing away those conversations into stealthy databases and mined for future patterns and trends. Trends on me, my lover and dog and cat.

So you don't owe Microsoft or Google or Apple anything. But it's in your best interest to learn how to live without them, for when they day of reckoning (perhaps by a lightning strike) finally comes, it'll come like a thief in the night.

Second Point:

You're a one man show. You and you alone are responsible for whatever outcome you find yourself in. Luck favors the prepared and you'll survive a storm far and away better if you prepare beforehand. Don't be the guy who thinks that good opsec involves bubble-gumming his 3.5 floppies to the duct work behind the vents in his room.

Third: Absolutes where good security is concerned don't exist. It's impossible to achieve 100% anonymity just as it's impossible to get 100% hack-proof data centers or 100% non-casualty rates on the battlefield no matter how good your opsec.

There's always a way in. There's always a leak, somewhere, waiting for a couple of fishermen to discover. A good security planner will weigh risk and apply his resources accordingly but good anonymity by way of phones, *especially cell phones*, comes down to who is trying to be anonymous from what and for how long. Disappearing from Google is not the same as disappearing from the NSA.

Take Tor, for instance. Tor is far easier to maintain anonymity on a laptop or PC using Linux than it ever will on Android. It's a nice enough tool but there are many apps that bleed your IP. Apps like those dealing with torrents.

If you're planning on using Tor on your phone to download torrents, stop reading. Return this book for a full refund. Other than clogging up the Tor network and making the Tor experience a rotten apple for other users, it is hell on anonymity services since it routes your REAL IP ADDRESS to destinations unknown. It does so anonymously of course, in the same way an envelope may be delivered by anonymous couriers. But with your real name and phone number on the inside of that envelope, well what's the point?

<u>The first basic tactic</u> is to change IP addresses, and do so <u>frequently</u>. Depending on the tool you use, most IP capable devices have the ability to set their own IP address. This tactic does come with a penalty though, because the frequent changing of IP addresses is highly anomalous. Depending on the internet service you're using at the time, it may be noted faster than you think. And if you're using Skype, well if they wanted to they could easily stream your voice to two locations at once, and there's nothing you can do to prevent that.

As well, any site that allows anonymous (or at least, accountless) posting can pretty much only block visitors by IPs. Then some of those people who got blocked are going to find a way to mask their IP (proxies, Tor, etc.) and get those IPs blocked too. Eventually you'll learn as I did that the problem isn't the websites, it's the jackasses that got them blocked. Your milage may vary.

The second basic tactic is to spoof and twin an IP address. With the first method you are using IP addresses that are valid for your local node, but are currently unused. For a 'spoof and twin' you want to use an IP address that another node is currently using. This method only works when your network adapter can be put into promiscuous mode and read traffic destined for other IP addresses. It requires that your device time transmission so as not to interfere with the target device, and that it continue reading open traffic until the target device receives a reply from whatever server you sent to.

Even if I provide you with the best available anonymity methods, if you are doing something that would attract the attention of law enforcement, those methods will only delay your eventual de-anonimization. Anyone with the capability of enlisting the help of large national or international telecommunication companies will find you in hours. That said, I will show you ways you could (in theory, say) prevent this event from happening. Read on.

8 DEADLY MYTHS OF CELL PHONES

We need to dispel a few myths before you learn how to go off the grid Michael Weston style. The first one is that smartphones are better at hiding you because of all the stealth apps available. It just isn't true.

Myth 1.) <u>Smartphones are better than older 'dummy' phones</u>.

Smarter, yes but better at hiding you? A very loud no with arms waving wildly. Consider for a moment why Russia decided to revert to typewriters after the NSA scandal broke over the German chancellor, Angela Merkel, found out that the NSA had been listening in on her calls for years. If you think it'd be much harder for any bureaucrat to spy on you if you reverted to 'the old methods', you'd be right.

Flip 'dummy' phones are superior to smartphones for good operational security, period. For any kind. They don't like to 'phone home' for one thing, and the less apps they support, the tighter your security. The reason for this is that most hacks and exploits target the most commonly used operating systems, like Windows and Android. And the 'superhackers' at the NSA love it when you use two dozen apps that you know little about. Take a hint from the Russians.

Myth 2.) <u>Home is safe as long as you're using Tor.</u>

Wrong again, a thousand times wrong. Home is a radioactive minefield as far as anonymity is concerned. Imagine yourself trying to handle a barrel of green radioactive goo without a protective suit. It's dangerously gooey stuff. Though I'll grant you'd survive it maybe long enough to call up HQ and tell them you botched the mission. Keep your phone somewhere distant even if all you want is to keep the wife out of your business. No need to leave a loaded gun around.

Myth 3.) <u>It doesn't matter where you activate your phone.</u>

Whenever I activate a phone, the opening scene from my favorite film, 'The Abyss', rolls in my head like an old film projector full of nostalgia and greasy engineers. One scene still haunts me to this day years after seeing it. It's that horrific opening scene where an underwater alien ship speeds too close to The Montana, a U.S. Navy nuclear-tipped submarine operating deep in the Cayman Trough in the Caribbean Sea.

The sleek, alien thing glides along at a whopping 130 knots. I still remember the Captain's words.

'Nothin' goes 130 knots!' he yells just as the power goes out.

The velocity of the alien ship knocks out almost every navigational instrument on the sub, sonar included. A few nail-biting seconds go by and when the power returns, the sub smashes nose first into a cliff and before anyone can breathe, the whole ship dives to the bottom of the ocean floor. But not before an officer launches the sub's emergency beacon.

That beacon breaches the surface in a flurry of little beeps and pulsing red light in the thick of midnight as ten foot waves crash all around. Picture a tiny red blip on a ten foot whitecap going Beep. Beep. BEEP. It's scary to think that the Navy found them. But find them they did.

It's not all that different when you activate your phone in any random place, where the **'activation'** itself will send such a signal to multiple parties interested in making your life, well, not very private at all. Maybe not *initially* mind you. It's the slow boiling frog scenario for most. First they'll want to know things like

- Where you live.
- Which sites you visit.
- What keywords you're punching into Google
- Where you're using your Mastercard.
- And who's related to you on all the social media sites.

All of this is tracked very quickly unless you've taken action beforehand to limit who gets this 'emergency beacon'. So how do we get around it? There's a few no so obvious ways.

One poor man's solution is to pay some starving English major at the local college ten bucks to activate it for you at a crowded college library you'll likely never visit. Be polite of course, but know that this fellow mustn't have any hard data on you except for any fake data you provide. If he starts asking questions, find some other urchin who isn't so nosy. Also know that this isn't the ideal solution. It just sets the stage for a very long process of *fogging up the trail*.

Myth 4.) <u>Untraceable Burners Can't Be Bought Online (at least not anonymously)</u>

This one is false as well. The problem with buying things on the Deep Web isn't that doing so requires you to be incognito. It's doing so without getting a lemon. You can in fact buy burners on the Deep Web (more on this later). For now know that one option is to use the Tor Browser Bundle to purchase anonymous burners, though like everything else on the deep web such as drugs, iPhones, Cuban cigars, you may be better off using *offline* proxies to purchase anything electronic. Chinese counterfeiting is popular on Darknet sites as you'll soon see. They fool enough buyers to leave glowing reviews at first, so it's buyer beware most of the time. That said, you can just as easily find a diamond in the rough offline.

Myth 5.) <u>Using Cash to Purchase Burners at Retail Stores is Always Anonymous</u>.

Little mom and pop stores are one thing, but big retail stores are truly privacy-hating places, especially where the Big Box Corporation has run off all the little shops in town. Those little shops made great places to forge alliances. That said, if you bought a burner from a big box store you should wait a month before you activate it. When I worked in security we'd rotate the footage daily, but did no firm deletions until 30 to 45 days out. You also must not be seen talking on-campus with that college English major we discussed. Again this depends on the level of opsec you require, but this is at a most basic, elementary level. We'll get more advanced as we go along.

Myth 6.) <u>No One Cares About Your Contact List</u>

Two things to say. The first is that contacts are *dangerous*. They create a pattern that, when lit up on a giant NSA screen, is like lighting a stick of dynamite with you being on the end of that stick. Boom again.

Much like a 'hidden' partition on a hard drive that stores two operating systems (one real and one fake a' la Veracrypt), you want to set up false leads to make it look like you have contacts where none exist. This fogs up your trail. One burner must not have the same contacts as the next. Any contacts provide less risk on paper than in a phone list since most SIM data will often give you away.

The second thing involves triangulation and pattern matching. Intelligence agencies favor "mirroring" devices over all others because of unique identifiers involved. Over time you can give yourself away by repeatedly using the same pattern, such as this:

House ---> Subway ---> Verizon (or your usual workplace) ---> Girlfriend's House ---> Home Again

Taking this route over and over establishes a mobility pattern. If anyone of importance comes looking for you, they'll find you whether you use a burner phone or not. The way to prevent this is to know your surroundings. Conversations are almost always the same length of time. That is, when talking with the same people in the same place.

Think about it. Your mother calls you on days when she doesn't work or when the hubby is at work, usually for the same 45 minute stretch. Your best friend John, probably 15-20 minutes since there's less emotional rambling. Men tend to not beat around the bush when talking other men, but over a month's time this creates a pattern of recognition if paired with other calls you make. All it takes is three or so matching patterns and it's game over.

Myth 7.) No One Cares About Broken Phones in Alleyways

Unless you want to go interrogating every bum from your home to the city limits, never throw out your phone 'as is', and especially not anywhere near your home. They should be securely wiped and then broken down piece by piece as though it were some ancient artifact belonging to some undead wizard.

Myth 8.) You're Anonymous on any Wireless Network (as long as you don't do anything stupid)

This is the most deadly myth. It has to do with using WiFi networks *securely*, and you wouldn't believe how many high school geeks think they're masters at Tor and hacking only to find the police show up because they threatened the wrong person online from the wrong dorm. On more than a few security sites, I see apps like Macspoofer and the like being recommended. Using any of these wonder-apps may prove detrimental to your freedom.

If your MAC address is in a constant state of identity crisis (or, always changing), you're narrowing the search parameters available to any adversary who wants to find you. For a group it draws massive unwanted attention. How? Because the access point is connected to multiple MAC numbers over a short period of time. It looks suspicious. Any administrator worth his salt will look into it. Better to look like everyone else rather than paint yourself black when surrounded by white sheep.

Mobile anonymity is difficult, frustrating, bothersome and generally a pain in the neck. Harder still is severing the link to your everyday life because depending on technology to do it all for you is a fool's game. A dead end. You need a good security mindset, diligence and the stamina to develop a *mental trigger* to predict accidents before they happen. We've all heard of what happens when a loaded gun is left on a table within arm's reach of a youngster. You need to anticipate this before it happens. To that, ask yourself the following:

Who do you need to hide from and why?

How much hard work and maintenance does it involve versus doing little?

Does it pass the effort to payoff test?

How much work is it to do it right versus getting caught and suffering the embarrassment of being under the spotlight and, heaven forbid, the family?

Whether you use Linux Mint or Windows 7 or a Mac, you need to kill any application if you entered any personal info into it that can aid in tracing you. Usernames that you used on forums should never be used in your anonymous phone or anonymous (like Linux Mint!) laptop.

Also, phone numbers, places of work, nicknames, hangouts, girls you've dated, online games - all of these are part of your real persona that leaves a trail right to your front door. That real persona needs to go into a coffin the moment the anonymous You comes out. Only then can we know ourselves well enough not to be bothered with worrying if we did everything correctly. By that time, we've done it so many times that it's an automatic timepiece in our subconscious. Do this and we'll see our true enemies more clearly, one of which is the NSA.

HOW THE NSA SPIES ON YOU

Let's say a few words on how the powers that be trace calls to begin with. It's a little technical but then it's always preferable to know what the enemy's capabilities.

If you're like me then you've probably rolled your eyeballs enough times whenever a bad guy on Burn Notice or CSI had twenty seconds or so to taunt the FBI before his location was traced. It's all baloney, and it happens in *every single cop show* on TV I've ever seen. They think we're lemmings. Well, many of us are.

The Rockford Files, CSI, and Burn Notice. I love every one of these shows but it just doesn't matter how much I love em because you can't love it when they get it wrong. And get it wrong they do aplenty. They get it wrong because the writers are not detectives themselves and many just want to get the script done asap, so they never shadow any in their day to day operations at all. But best-selling authors like James Patterson do their homework. Go figure.

Phone signals came inline some forty years ago and back then how you got connected was very different than today. A call was setup from one switch to the next, and the next, and then the next until finally a connecting-circuit relayed your voice.

These days most switches are simultaneous since most calls are over SS7 (that is, the Signaling System which manages calls). Each calling station is traceable at the beginning too, so the trace countdown you see on most cop shows really does stretch the truth. But it makes for a suspenseful police drama and, let's face it, most people don't mind suspending disbelief for an hour if they can get good entertainment.

I've trouble doing this though. Perhaps I'm just an impatient guy when it comes to police procedural shows but one episode on CSI came across as gut-wrenchingly sloppy. It showed a low-level programmer realigning a satellite from his laptop *without any assistance from any other agency*. I nearly fell out of my chair. It takes an insane amount of teamwork and coordination between other agencies to do something of that technical caliber.

Mobile phone tracing does require more resources than a landline since a cell phone number is not connected to a single switch. But it isn't impossible for a mobile phone provider to locate which towers the phone used or what region the call was made. One way of doing it is by comparing signal strength and then correlating that with the antenna that held your signal. If you've got an unencrypted non-burner phone, the GPS chip inside will give up your location to any who are in possession of it.

I bet you're wondering how come you can't trace a mobile phone like your cell phone company can.

The reason is the same reason that you can't identify individuals by IP address alone. Only the telephone company knows because they have the logs. They own the equipment. They have easy access. Even police need a subpoena to get subscriber access from a VPN, (or virtual private network). They can't hack the system for one individual without risking their job (or political career). Well, the NSA can I suppose, only that's a whole other enchilada. But for the internet itself no node within it is any more special than any of the others since it uses the same band.

Unlike phones.

Wait a second, you say. If that's true, then how am I supposed to prevent my phone from being tracked?

The short answer is: You can't without the right opsec *and* the right mindset. If you're using towers then you can be traced, generally speaking. But this isn't a perfect world and those towers aren't perfect either. They produce false positives just like our anti-virus programs do, albeit differently. But you can toy with the triangulation angle a bit to obfuscate the trail.

One method involves using a PBX system to delay identity discovery. Notice I said *delay*, not eradicate. The way to do it is to connect with a company's PBX system via dial-up. This will have them looking in the wrong spot. It's still possible for them to trace you given enough time but not without going though the company logs. That takes time too and to be honest they'd rather not bother unless ordered to do so by a higher power.

You can also do it by creating false leads using radio waves (yes, a radio) that links your voice to your phone. Do it right and the guy who is chasing you will end up chasing the wind. You can set the signal to whatever you want. A hundred feet becomes a half a mile and now Mr. Smith's area to catch you has suddenly become much larger. Much larger means more time, more money and more resources.

However, neither of the above methods mean anything if you are either one of three things:

- Lax with your metadata (i.e. those you regularly contact).
- Lax with your situational awareness.
- Lax with opsec.

THE NSA FINGERPRINTS

Bob from accounting claims one burner is as good as the next. Tom agrees somewhat, but insists you need a voodoo doll and a crazy formula he read on an Ars Technica thread to really make it anonymous. The new girl in programming, one sexy Carrie-Anne, insists it's really what you do outside of a phone that matters. Whom do we trust? Bob the Yes Man, Tom the Tax Expert or the goth-chick-turned-hacker Carrie-Anne? What is 'good enough' anyway?

It depends on where you are. One burner can be as good as the next in Southeast Asia if that's where you're headed. Or it may be 'good enough' if you're trekking to the South Pole or diving in some bombed out Japanese sub off the Philippines and aren't really hiding from anyone except Great White sharks.

But Bangkok and the Philippines aren't North America or the UK. It's tough defeating towering bullies over small badgers though both pose a serious threat. I know because

I've tried – and failed. When you get right down to it, it mostly depends on who you're trying to hide from.

But regardless of who that 'someone' is, there are two main types of cell technology we can work with. The first is GSM, which stands for Global System for Mobiles, and CDMA which stands for Code Division Multiple Access.

You and I can't cross them, which is why I can't use my AT&T cell on Verizon's service. Most of the major carriers make it simple for LEOs to trace calls because they separate burner phone traffic from prepaid traffic. A Sprint executive may say it's because they need to prioritize traffic. Only what he doesn't tell you is that it's used by the NSA and law enforcement to track down 'anonymous' callers.

The NSA does this by 'fingerprinting' every call. Fingerprint analysis is based on the contacts unique to each caller. That is, *your* unique contacts, as well as how long you talk to those contacts and how long they talk to *their* contacts. It all adds up to a nice fat profile on you that is shady at best and outright evil at worst.

Let's say our friend Jerry talks to Kramer, George and Elaine every day as he sits down with his Wheaties. He has several phones, different carriers, only the info he adds per 'Friend' per contact makes for one helluva traceable target. Every bit of data on these contacts (that is, Kramer, George & Elaine) are placed on the SIM card and match the exact contact data on any other burner he uses. For federal law enforcement to track him down would be laughably easy.

For the NSA, a few clicks in the Prism system and from there it'd be no effort at all to find his geographical location.

Location, Location, Location

So then, how to solve this problem? Well first we need to define what 'location' really means to the Big Data players.

Carriers like Verizon store data based on your phone's signal-strength. That is, the 'weight' of your call between you and the nearest cell tower. It stores a mind-boggling amount of numerical data on your behavior and, at the simplest level, this is known as 'triangulation' locating. The GPS functions in your phone use it more often than you realize. Apps like Google Earth and Maps.Me use it as much as they can and provide your whereabouts to distant servers - and as a side hustle bonus are better able to target you with ads based on that data. It's a real juicy side of income if you've got Google's or the NSA's data centers to sort it all out.

The second thing to note is the Christmas Day error. Come one wintry Christmas morning when the cardinals and sparrows flutter about in the snowy front yard, you open your presents to find a fancy smartphone, one loaded with gizmo after gizmo. It cost a fortune and you can't wait to hit the ignition. What's the first thing you do? What's the first thing *anyone* does?

They'll call up that number to activate it. Lickety split.

They're way too sloshed to realize it, but doing that is like a tipsy mouse nibbling a morsel of cheese in a trap with the cat watching from the cover of darkness.
    Before they can kick back another shot of Jack Daniels and eggnog, they blurt out their full name, home address

and their mistress's password in front of the wife. From that point on it's near impossible to spoof anything because of the correlation of that phone with their real location - and all the locations and profiles of every phone user in the house. Why do they need your contact list now that you've connected to everyone in your household?

And it ain't just the NSA either.

HOW THE IRS SPIES ON YOU

It's not just the NSA that uses Stingray surveillance technology to spy on the citizenry. The IRS now uses it as well to capture metadata from cell phones. They're a part of the Big Data empire too, and they demand only the best tools of the trade: the most expensive *and* the most invasive. They use something known as *IMSI interceptors* (or cell site simulators).

Worse, IRS agents now have the same authority previously held only by judges. This power gives them authority to install Pen register devices so they can spy on people they suspect aren't giving their fair share. Or anyone that challenges them for that matter.

Historically, these were used by the FBI to capture recordings by Mafia members or Mexican Cartel leaders in Juarez. You know, real criminals. Nowadays everyone with a U.S. passport is fair game and if they run out of real criminals to prosecute, well by golly they'll just invent a few more to keep the the gravy train running full-steam. There's even rumors flying that student loan defaulters will have their passports revoked. Not too far fetched since they do the same with child support obligations, and that's only $2500, not $50,000.

Anyway. From the eagle's viewpoint you can see the IRS' Stingrays are high-tech doppelgangers. They are clones of a cell tower that can force any phone within reach to silently connect so that any metadata can be siphoned off.

Kinda like one of those parasites you see in PBS nature documentaries, where the plant benefits and the parasite benefits in a kind of symbiosis that's a pain to study in a college textbook but fun to watch. Only where the IRS is concerned, the benefits flow in one direction only.

The kicker? That parasite will die far sooner than the plant. Think on this for a moment. What do you think's going to happen if your country suddenly finds itself unable to borrow from anyone? If you've studied history you already know the answer. They steal their own citizens' wealth in a very, well, parasitic-like way. We've seen this in Argentina, Poland and France.

Don't believe for a minute the IRS will only be using this spy tech on the millionaire fat cats living abroad. Those guys are small potatoes. If they were to seize every fatcat's funds in every country on Earth, it'd be enough to pay for Medicare for a scant 3 years. Then they'd be right back where they started. If you don't believe it then allow me to quote a rather well-known statesman on this topic:

"If you will not fight for right when you can easily win without blood shed; if you will not fight when your victory is sure and not

too costly; you may come to the moment when you will have to fight with all the odds against you and only a precarious chance of survival. There may even be a worse case. You may have to fight when there is no hope of victory, because it is better to perish than to live as slaves."

- Winston S. Churchill

HOW GOOGLE SPIES ON YOU

Google loves you to death. They love everyone actually, or more to the point, everyone's private data. There's gold in them ones and zeros and most people offer em up quite willingly for their daily digital fix.

Google loves to store data about you when you're not looking. That's what happens when you invite a vampire into your home. Tough as nails to kick out and they leave a trail of confusion and mayhem when they finally do hightail it. Like little cousin Eddie whose long since outlived his welcome.

As a fairly strong privacy advocate, I like to manage that online privacy by controlling the data I make available online. The problem is that Google's been getting smarter at meta-managing me by my own keywords on other search engines. The only option is to enact whatever privacy controls are required yourself. Or don't use any of Google's services. And that my friend is a very long list that includes:

Google Search
    Gmail
    Google Plus
    Google Alerts
    Google Books
    Google Finance
    Google Groups
    Google Hotel Finder
    Google Flight Search
    Google Translate
    Google Trends
    Life Search (or Google China)
    ... and a host of others.

The master list of course is a lot longer. The data-mining operations for each of these services cost millions each day. Google's algorithm tries to predict what you'll want tomorrow or next Christmas. That's fine with some people because it's legal after all and they've been doing that since forever.

The problem is that they share this with any government who pays them or allows them entry into the country. This becomes a problem overseas if you need to use online storage. Enter Google Drive.

Google Drive

Google Drive makes for one helluva solution for business travelers who need to protect sensitive files from cross-border guards. Guard who love to confiscate laptops and pen drives because, well, they want to look competent.

    Just upload the data to Big G before you hit the US

border and you're good to go. This also works if you have to travel to out of the way places like Philippines.

Well, most of the time. So what's the problem then?

Google is the problem, just as iCloud was a problem for a few celebrities who got hacked. It happens every year. Just ask Jennifer Lawrence how she feels about tossing her pics 'in the cloud' after her nudes got hacked and leaked. There's plenty of other risks too:

- Law enforcement can access it with a judge-signed warrant.

- The NSA can give the FBI full access to your files.

- Any alphabet agency can access it. Agencies like the DEA, ATF, CIA, & the IRS *if* they have the NSA's ability to bypass Google's encryption (which Google only beefed up after the media revealed that the NSA was siphoning data from their tailpipe.)

- Employees may upload personal info in the cloud which, if hacked, cause financial issues and maybe even a lawsuit.

- Any bank you deal with may deny you any reimbursement of lost funds if you store bank details in the cloud. They'll consider it 'negligence' on your part.

It's more effective to use an encryption app like Veracrypt or PGP to *work with* Google Drive. What I do is:

- First fire up Veracrypt or Truecrypt 7.1a
    - Create a storage file,
    - Pick 2 algo-based encryption schemes with SHA-512 keys
    - Put all my sensitive files in there.
    - Then and only then do I upload the encrypted files to Google Drive.

When I need to alter my work, say update a new draft of a novel I'm working on but don't want Google scanning it for 'offending' terms, I just copy the encrypted doc out of Google Drive, update it and then re-encrypt and re-upload to Google Drive. If I ever want to delete it, I just delete the encrypted storage file. It's easy peasy and it'll be eons before Google has Skynet's quantum computers to crack the encryption key.

Encryption and Google

As I mentioned, any governmental agency can and will access your cloud storage via a subpoena sent to Google. But what are the consequences if law enforcement confiscates your phone? Your laptop? It happens. And as it so happens you may be arrested on a totally separate case but they've insufficient evidence.

Except your laptop and phone are now in their hands. Here are the risks, number one of which is:

- Doppelgangers. Enemy numero uno. Any login cookies for Google services (like Google Docs)

- can be copied to impersonate you, or they can login to all Google accounts in Firefox or Chrome and act as the Real You.

- They can steal your password from the browser's password storage file if you've no master password set.

- And with your password they can reset it in Google and all Google services.

- Chrome might cache parts of files or documents the last time you logged in.

- Or they can use Data Recovery Tools to retrieve your deleted files.

You can avoid each of the above scenarios by using a full-disk encryption program. As long as your phone or laptop is powered off when they take it (and you're not in a jurisdiction where they can beat the password out of you), you're safe as long as the country in question respects your right to remain silent.

As for a searching solution that replaces Google outright, I use and recommend DuckDuckGo. It's not as laser-refined as Google is, but they must operate exactly as advertised. One thing they're very clear on is their privacy policy, which states:

- They don't track you.
- They don't sell your search data to other websites
- They don't require cookies.

- They don't collect metadata on you
- They don't store your search history.

It's black and white without a lot of legalese that most people just skip through anyway. Clear and plain as day. If they ever decide to embrace the dark side (as Google has) then the FTC can file a lawsuit. The main thing is that if a company has a privacy policy, then they must *stick to it*. No matter what.

Google Chrome

Google Chrome's a lot like Stephen King's Christine, a 1957 Plymouth Fury who loves it's owner a bit too much. She runs fast and hot and horny and like that hellspawn of a car, Chrome'll resist any temptation to tinker, mod or otherwise tighten her steel gaped maw because she thinks she can do the job better than you can. Besides, why should she take orders from some lowly peon, anyway?

But I'll tell you how it all ends: It ends with the kid owner paying a high price for putting a speed demon ahead of his family. Chrome, like Christine, 'repairs' herself without permission a little too often for my liking.

She's certainly fast though, just like Christine. But she's not that fast. And there are some serious consequences to not looking under the hood. Here are a few gems that are considered 'benefits' to the end user by Google:

- Each web url you type is sent to Google for the auto complete function - without telling you.

- Each file you download gets sent to the Big G too. They verify it against a master 'white list' then link your IP address to that file for months.
- Chrome checks every hour on the hour a list of blacklisted URLs to 'protect' you. Even opening Chrome tells Google where you are.
- When you logon to Google Gmail, they know everything about your browser: Tabs, History & all Bookmarks. Then they store it in one of those giant data centers of theirs.
- Will load a site before you finish the address.

Remember: If you are getting it for free, you are not the customer. You are the product.

HOW WINDOWS SPIES ON YOU

Windows 10 is the flagship of Microsoft's cloud-centric vision, and written under the hood is the hope that you'll one day depend on that cloud for more than just accessing game saves. In the meantime, Windows 10 is not a particularly happy operating system unless it's looking online for drivers updates, patches and the like for your supposed benefit. It wants to put a smile on your face.

It all sounds well and good until the real goal becomes apparent: looking for people who fit your own social circle and 'buying' habits and corralling everyone into a nice trackable pen... all without asking you first.

Yes, I know. Microsoft's spying on the masses is hardly news. It's old hat and they're not the only ones doing it by a long shot. Every company you give money to channels your money into some kind of marketing analysis with the laser sights focused somehow on you and your stuff. Supermarkets like Winn-Dixie or Wal-Mart use them to such a laser-refined edge that they know when your daughter is pregnant before you do. It seems like a decent man just can't escape this dragnet without going off-grid and living like

Jeremiah Johnson (I've tried that too, and failed spectacularly when I ran into a grizzly. More on that later).

But let's not fall on our sword just yet. You *can* in fact escape any chance of law enforcement, governments or hackers getting a hold of that data, and that's our aim, as when your data is shared with governments or criminals that abuse this information, well, a lot of nasty surprises come down the pike. Below is Microsoft's privacy statement and FAQ regarding the Diagnostics Tracking Service that comes with Windows 10:

"As you use Windows, we collect performance and usage information that helps us identify and troubleshoot problems as well as improve our products and services. We recommend that you select Full for this setting."

- Full data includes all Basic and Enhanced data, and also turns on advanced diagnostic features that collect additional data from your device, such as system files or memory snapshots, which may unintentionally include parts of a document you were working on when a problem occurred. This information helps us further troubleshoot and fix problems. If an error report contains personal data, we won't use that information to identify, contact, or target advertising to you. This is the recommended option for the best Windows experience and the most effective troubleshooting.

Them's Microsoft's words, not mine, and note also that only on Enterprise Edition can one turn Diagnostics Tracking Service off completely. Diagnostics Tracking Service consists of these files:

telemetry.asm-windowsdefault.json
diagtrack.dll
utc.app.json
utcresources.dll

It's not likely anyone can lockdown Windows 10 enough to know what they send or don't send either by laptop, PC or cell phone. As Ars Technica has found out, it's impossible to know why Windows 10 can't seem to stop talking to Microsoft's servers. Furthermore, Windows takes system files or <u>memory snapshots</u>, which may inadvertently include PARTS OF A DOCUMENT YOU WERE WORKING ON when a problem occurred. Note that Android isn't much different. It has a similar data collection policy as does Mac OS.

<u>Windows Privacy Settings</u>

Windows 10 comes with some privacy settings turned on and some turned off. You can open up the Settings app and tic off what you like or don't, but know that they're all tied to your Unique Advertising Identifier. This Identifier is shared across other apps you use to allow Microsoft to spy on you and show you targeted ads in much the same way Wal-Mart does with your Sam's Club card. Corporations share this with each other and some sell it outright for truckloads of cash - as do Search engines like Bing and Google. With Bing Search sitting there in the start menu, you can bet you rubber-flesh copy of Evil Dead that any search queries will not stay private. They'll be outed just as if you typed them into Bing itself. Even URLs get sent to Microsoft for validation purposes so it goes without saying that some cellar doors should remain shut. Permanently.

CORTANA

Cortana comes with Windows 10 automatically enabled after install. With this on you consent to Microsoft to grant a personal assistant of sorts, one that'll send data about your activities (including applications you run, GPS locations, browsing history) back and forth between your PC and Microsoft. It also includes your handwriting and voice imprint. You can disable these within Speech, Inking & Typing within Privacy settings, but know that Cortana isn't unique in this kind of privacy abuse, as Google Now and Siri do the same thing.

It should be obvious that this is a Very Bad Thing if you plan on doing anything remotely shady on the Deep Web. If you absolutely must use Windows 10 (which I strongly recommend you do not), you must -above all else- disable *data logging*. Here's how.

DISABLE DATA LOGGING IN WINDOWS 10

A few of these fixes are a bit overkill, and if you're not sure what to do then stick to the "before installation" and "after installation" parts. DON'T start mucking about with the Powershell or the registry editor if you don't have at least a good idea of what you're doing though. This goes a bit farther than merely being 'computer literate', obviously, but it illustrates how dangerous Windows really is to anonymity.

BEFORE/DURING INSTALLATION

Do not use Express Settings. Hit Customize, and make sure everything is turned off. It's strongly preferred that you use a local account with Windows 10.

AFTER INSTALLATION

Head to Settings > Privacy, and disable everything, unless there are some things you really need. While within the Privacy page, go to Feedback, select Never in the first box, and Basic in the second box.

Head to Settings > Update and Security > Advanced Options > Choose how updates are delivered, and turn the first switch off.

Disable Cortana by right clicking the Search bar/icon.

(Optional) Disable web search in Search by going to Settings, and turning off Search online and include web results.

Getting More Complex

Open up the Command Prompt by launching CMD as an administrator (hit windows key or click start menu button, type "cmd" then right click on the command prompt icon at the top of the list and select "run as administrator"), then enter the following:

sc delete DiagTrack

sc delete dmwappushservice

echo "" > C:\ProgramData\Microsoft\Diagnosis ETLLogs-AutoLogger\AutoLogger-Diagtrack-Listener.etl

Open up the Group Policy Editor by launching gpedit.msc as an administrator (same method as cmd).

Go through Computer Configuration > Administrative Templates > Windows Components > Data Collection and Preview Builds. Double click Telemetry, hit Disabled, then apply.

While still in the Group Policy Editor, go through Computer Configuration > Administrative Templates > Windows Components > OneDrive, double click Prevent the usage of OneDrive for file storage, hit Enabled, then apply.

Open up the Registry Editor by launching regedit as an administrator (yet again same method as cmd).

Go through HKEY_LOCAL_MACHINE\SOFTWARE\Microsoft\Windows\CurrentVersion\Policies\DataCollection, select AllowTelemetry, change its value to 0, then apply.

First, download the Take Ownership tweak: http://www.howtogeek.com/howto/windows-vista/add-take-ownership-to-explorer-right-click-menu-in-vista/ and enable it.

Then, head to the Hosts File by going to C:\Windows\System32\Drivers\Etc,

and take ownership of the hosts file, then add the following IPs into it (using notepad or whatever text editor you prefer).

127.0.0.1 vortex.data.microsoft.com

127.0.0.1 vortex-win.data.microsoft.com

127.0.0.1 telecommand.telemetry.microsoft.com

127.0.0.1 telecommand.telemetry.microsoft.com.nsatc.net

127.0.0.1 oca.telemetry.microsoft.com

127.0.0.1 oca.telemetry.microsoft.com.nsatc.net
127.0.0.1 sqm.telemetry.microsoft.com
127.0.0.1 sqm.telemetry.microsoft.com.nsatc.net
127.0.0.1 watson.telemetry.microsoft.com
127.0.0.1 watson.telemetry.microsoft.com.nsatc.net
127.0.0.1 redir.metaservices.microsoft.com
127.0.0.1 choice.microsoft.com
127.0.0.1 choice.microsoft.com.nsatc.net
127.0.0.1 df.telemetry.microsoft.com
127.0.0.1 reports.wes.df.telemetry.microsoft.com
127.0.0.1 services.wes.df.telemetry.microsoft.com
127.0.0.1 sqm.df.telemetry.microsoft.com
127.0.0.1 telemetry.microsoft.com
127.0.0.1 watson.ppe.telemetry.microsoft.com
127.0.0.1 telemetry.appex.bing.net
127.0.0.1 telemetry.urs.microsoft.com
127.0.0.1 telemetry.appex.bing.net:443
127.0.0.1 settings-sandbox.data.microsoft.com
127.0.0.1 vortex-sandbox.data.microsoft.com
127.0.0.1 telemetry.*

Additional Fixes:

Replace Microsoft Edge/Internet Explorer with Firefox, Chromium, or any forks/variations you want. Note however that if you install Chrome, you're just choosing to have your data stolen by Google instead of Microsoft if you're surfing naked (i.e. without Tor).

Replace Windows Media Player with VLC or MPC-HC.

Replace Groove Music with Foobar2000, Winamp, or MusicBee.

Replace Photos/Windows Photo Viewer with ImageGlass or IrfanView.

Some of you are shaking your heads at this, and I agree with your assessment that this barely scratches the surface of what Microsoft's nefarious operating system is capable of doing. This plugs just a few holes but there are just too many to fill if you need rock-solid anonymity. For this reason alone you should use Linux (Tor with Tails) if at all possible.

HOW TO TELL IF YOUR PHONE IS TAPPED

A phone tapped with a keylogger is a bomb waiting to go off since the keylogger secretly records (and emails) every username and password you type in. Keyloggers aren't foolproof though. There are a few signs that may give clues that it isn't just your eyes seeing the screen.

1.) Unexplained Data Spikes - Are there any unusual spikes in the size of data being stored on the device? A lot of spyware programs pack data under the hood when you're not looking so it can be sent out later in bulk. Efficient spy payload you might call it. My Data Manager is good at monitoring this but the best spyware apps will evade detection since the footprint is becoming ever smaller and the size of devices ever bigger.

2.) Unusual Phone Activity - Things like turning itself off or your lock screen suddenly flashing on when you're not using it.

3.) Line Noise - If you're in the Philippines and making calls, line stability is often terrible in provincial areas like Davao or Dumaguete. That means tons of noise. If you're in a first world nation, a constant stream of 'clicks' and 'beeps' can signal that someone, somewhere, is listening.

4.) Encrypted Emails - This can happen with poorly designed spyware, where you receive odd messages that make no sense and are filled with strange symbols. Spy applications are known to be buggy little critters and not even keyloggers used by the FBI to capture keystrokes of mafia members are perfect.

5.) Odd Files in Directories - It's often easy to see spyware's been installed on your device by just looking into a few subdirectories on your Android or iPhone. Often I find if I do a Google search for the name of the file, someone somewhere has likewise found this exact same file. Better still is that they've opened a forum thread asking for help. Most of the time the file turns out to be quite old. This saves me the trouble of using expensive forensic software like Paraben's Device Seizure or UFED Physical Analyzer.

HOW TO STAY ANONYMOUS OVERSEAS

You've won the Powerball lottery and Uncle Sam awaits his cut. Problem is, so are some ugly long lost relatives who've managed to track you down and are now throwing down an epic guilt trip by sleeping in a van next to your mailbox. They're threatening to sleep down by the river too.

But that's not all. A guy named Eddie you remember from 3rd grade claims to have been your best friend. Except that he really wasn't. All you remember is that he gave you back a chewed up No. 2 pencil that looked fresh out of the hamster bin at the pet store.

You need to get away from this heat. Settle down somewhere and let things simmer down so you can think and restrategize. So you take aim and throw a dart at a world map on the wall and it lands smack dab in the middle of Zamboanga, Philippines. You hop on Google Earth and think, my my, it looks an awful lot like Maui. Then you get all googly-eyed at those turquoise-watered beaches.

Only it isn't quite that. There's a few terrorists walking around (real ones, not the old grannies the TSA likes to pull aside to interrogate).

What could possibly go wrong?

To be honest, everything. You're a walking ATM in the Philippines and most of the locals know it, though by how much is debatable. But they all think you're rich. If you can afford a $1500 round-trip flight at the other end of the world well then you're as rich as Trump in their liquid green eyes. Now, not everyone is looking to rip you off mind you, but the cab drivers certainly will and if you're in Zambooanga, watch out because that's the danger zone of all danger zones.

Americans, British citizens and Canadians alike are kidnapped routinely whenever they venture too far into Mindanao territory. Especially Zamboanga. You'd never know Zamboanga houses terrorists because it looks like Cebu and even Manila. How safe are those cities? Not very. For this reason you better get ready to lie your tail off before you ever set foot on a plane. Nice guys get killed over there. Quickly.

The first thing you need is a Fake Name. No way around it. You have to know your lies inside and out before you're airborne. Then you need to build a foundation to support this lie in the event you're discovered. We'll use Philippines as an example since that's where our dart landed and also because it's the most socially networked country in the world, bar none. And I don't mean online.

1.) First things first, make up an email account using first name.last name@whereever.com. The name should obviously be fake and be something common to your country but not to your city. So if you're from Chinatown you better pick someplace else. John Smith is perhaps too obvious for most tall white guys. You must never use this email for any connections to your real name because the aim here is to muddy the trail when anyone goes looking for the real you.

They'll perform reverse-image searches, phone numbers, white pages, and maybe even Usenet and Ars Technica forums looking for your favorite Skype nicknames.

Never let this fake name connect to social media that's connected to the real you. Ever. As well, never use this name on the same IP address if you can help it. Use a VPN on a laptop specific to this fake name. Signup for Facebook if you must but realize that if you login from the same IP address as your Real You, Facebook will know it and will broadcast it to the world.

2.) Women will almost always ask 'Is that your real name?' when they talk to you on Skype or some other chatroom. IF you have to you can tell them you work for the CIA or that you're the next Stephen King and your publisher's threatened to string you up from the nearest tree if you reveal your real name. If anyone online asks for an address, sever all communications immediately. They're likely either a stalker or an identity thief.

3.) Listed here are the primary things that'll give up the goose: airport luggage with your real name on it, business cards, laptops, tablets, iPhones with your real life pictures of you as a baby scattered about, and receipts. Anything in your wallet is a dead giveaway unless you have a prearranged DECOY wallet. A professional liar's wallet.

4.) Never post old photos to a fake Facebook page. Any photos have to be made exclusively for that profile and nothing else lest they see old photos from your real Facebook page.

5.) A problem area is check-in at the Marriot with a nice girl at your side, the same you just lied to. Only the cute emerald-green eyed girl at the desk asks for your real name. Do you lie? That breaks your cover. How about holding up an ID card? Nope again. She could easily ask you to pronounce it because not everyone there speaks perfect English. So now your goose is cooked. What to do, what to do.

Well for starters you can reserve a room by phone beforehand and not online. She'll ask for ID no matter what so you have to be ready. That means:

- Preparing a business card beforehand with your website and fake email and hand it to whoever asks. Just don't act nervous giving it out or you'll find out like Jim Rockford did in the 70s that bad liars are an embarrassment to everyone involved, so be as supercool as Mr. Orange was in Reservoir Dogs.

- Put everything with your real ID in a safe in the room. Passports too (you did email yourself a copy in the event it's stolen, right? Those Pinoy trikes have a lot of sticky fingers). If she or he asks what's in the safe just say the next War and Peace manuscript. Gold to you but worthless to them.

- Only put your fake email on your luggage tags, not your real name.

- Duct-tape your passport and a few hundred dollars to the inside of your suitcase lining. Sew it back up so the baggage handlers don't get suspicious.

- Ensure the 'location' feature of any phone is turned off. You shouldn't even bring a phone like this but for the sake of argument there was once a pinay who could see that was on E 85th and 3rd. She was a few blocks off but close enough to see where I was staying.

THE 10 BEST PHONES FOR ANONYMITY

Admittedly, smartphones and burner phones can mean different things to different people depending on the laws of their respective countries. Sometimes a burner is just a prepaid phone to Joe survivalist: cheap and good to go for when a natural disaster strikes. It'll get the job done. But that isn't the case with Fred the ex-CIA guy. The word smartphone is a bit of a misnomer too, like 'cat owner', because in reality the phone will own *you* if you get sloppy with your opsec.

ONE ADVANTAGE that you want in a burner is being able to ditch it *fast*. Prepaid doesn't always fall into this category. So you need to be clear at the outset what you intend to do if the heat gets too hot. Plan B, to say.

DITCH IT IN THE RIVER? But ditching a Blackphone near to where you live may get you a longer sentence than actually handing it over to the police. For this reason it can really pay to invest in good mobile security. But first let's run through a couple of sloppy scenarios so you have an idea of what not to do.

Scenario #1: Bad Weed

All weed is bad if the opsec is bad. But let's say it isn't and we live in a perfect world where everything goes according to plan. Let's say you buy a burner phone that Otto the bus driver recommended. He wants a bag of weed. You commit to it. You buy it on the Deep Web and do so far away from home. You then dispose of it and consider that number 'burned'. Okay then, that seems smart enough. Only what works for the Deep Web doesn't fly so straight on riskier outlets. Outlets like Craigslist.

AFTER GETTING that bag of reefer, you get a sales itch. You've smoked the bag yourself and figure to get another one only when you do you're as high as Tommy Chong and order another round using a non-burner with ties to your real number on the clearnet. You used a burner, true enough. But not an isolated burner. You accessed Tor using your real phone. Now you're not only at risk of an LE arrest, but the sheer number of certifiable psychos out there that make Quint from Jaws look like Pollyanna may just show up on your doorstep because you used a credit card over Tor. Not smart.

Scenario #2: Bad Dates, Good Dates

Burners make excellent date screeners too. No, not the date Indiana Jones came close to swallowing. I mean romantic dates. You save yourself tons of hassle using a burner in case the date goes sour and you believe you should part ways amicably (but the other party doesn't). A burner number thus can be untraceable, rendering any stalker a non-threat - as long as you didn't invite them to your house.

WE'RE NOT interested in buying a burner for dating, obviously. We're interested in what it'd take to get away with buying something on the Black Market in a country that doesn't like Black Markets. You know, a control thing, the peasants vs. The Man. So as you flip through these phones you need to ask yourself if you can handle the heat that'd come down if your identity happened to be compromised.

- If you're a vendor of big crates of contraband (crates filled with those little green Toy Story aliens which are filled with, uh, green stuff), even the high-tech super spy Blackphone will be of little use since if you're pulled over by the cops, they're bound to bring a sniffer dog that'll give the a-okay to strip your car to the bone. They'll find something. They don't need the burner (though granted it'd be nice to see your customer list - any one of which will rat you out).

- Ditch your Glock before your encrypted phone. Getting caught with a handgun while dealing *anything* shady is like getting caught with one in

Canada. They'll throw away the key after they throw you in a cell with snow gremlins.

- Cops love 'knock and talks'. That's when they just want to have a 'little chat' to get you to incriminate yourself. Never answer the door if they knock. If they have a warrant they'll likely come in anyway and bombard you with questions while they search. And on that topic, always, always make sure all your lights work before driving. Otherwise expect a 'talk' on the interstate.

- Get a legal side hustle, hobby, or side dream to shoot for. With straight-shooting friends. If you engage the cops for a living to feed your kids, say selling guns to rival gang members or even those granny biker gangs from Fury Road, you'll do serious time sooner or later. Lady luck favors those with more to lose.

- Never, ever break two laws at the same time.

- Bragging can get you 20 years due to this little thing called 'gossip' - your uncle Spanky, your siblings, your girlfriend. More on the finer details of Dark Personas in later chapters.

- If you're the best business in town then people will talk. Your name will be passed around to undesirables. Burner phones cannot prevent this.

BLACKPHONE

I.) Blackphone

Designed by an entrepreneur, a technology expert, a cryptographer and a former Navy SEAL, the Blackphone does just what it claims to do. It protects you from the prying eyes of the NSA and a few more of its Big Data brothers. Unfortunately this protection comes at a high price: $629. Not cheap. But for rock-solid security you could do a lot worse.

It uses PrivatOS, an operating system that gives you 100% control over who or what an app talks to. Another plus is the preventative measures that kick in when you power it on: Protection from hackers and identity thieves or just some back-alley kid whose eying your phone in Wendy's like Gollum's fishing buddy.

The specs are as follows:

Screen Size: 4.7" (1280 * 720)

Display Technology: 4.7" IPS HD
Technology: Capacitive >4 point multi-touch

Camera

Sensor size main camera 8 MP AF
Type of camera flash: Flash LED
Front camera 5MP FF

Connectivity

Single micro-SIM slot
Bluetooth Class 4.0 LE
Wi-Fi 802.11b/g/n
Micro USB
3.5mm audio jack

Hardware

Processor: Quad-core 2GHz System on Chip (SoC)
Platform: NVIDIA Tegra 4i

Need a good camera to give to a scout in enemy territory? Try the Blackphone's 8 megapixel rear cam. It's not top of the line but then the front cam is 5 megapixels and 16GB internal storage, so it's sufficient for surveillance work. The other plus is the CPU: an Nvidia Tegra 4i chip.

As a rule most cameras aren't terribly friendly to privacy to begin with, considering the metadata available within the images. Then there's the GPS stamps. But the device has to be compromised before it can be abused. If it's compromised, anything else you do on the device is no longer private anyway.

So how anonymous is it? The short answer is *very anonymous*. But like I said, it's pricey, but at what cost security? To that I'd say that as far as anonymity goes all the apps bundled with the device (if you bought them individually) would cost you more than the phone itself. Things like:

- an included 1 year membership to Silent Suite

- A 1-year "Friends and Family" Silent Circle Subscription

- 1 year of encrypted web browsing from Disconnect, 1GB/month

- 1 year of secure cloud backup from SpiderOak, 5GB/month

It also has the ability to remote wipe. The PrivatOS got this one right.

Granted you have to create an account for this to work. But it's like holding a handheld nuclear launch code device. If your phone's been stolen, if you've loaned it to Harry whose been suspiciously absent from meetings for the last few days, or your sister 'borrowed' it and loaned it to her best friend's golf partner's brother-in-law, then fire and forget. Remote Wipe is a dream option.

There's also the **Kismet Smarter WiFi Manager**. This app memorizes your trusted networks by triangulating cell towers within the area. It comes preconfigured to make any kind of spoofing of your network very very difficult. If you travel out of any established circle of 'trusted networks', the app turns off WiFi and your MAC address.

Since the app can turn off WiFi that means you won't be broadcasting your home network name to every Joe Schmo within earshot. Lots of random attacks by bored hackers and script kiddies tend to undo people who don't care. If they know your network's name they can spoof it and begin running all kinds of scripts that sniff every byte of your traffic. That leads a trail to your front door.

If you bite the bullet and purchase this, check out the Disconnect Secure Wireless service, a VPN that encrypts everything you do online. What this app does is send all traffic via proxy to kill any tracking data inserted into, say, Supercookies. One click and done.

Two other must-have apps come preinstalled. They are:

- Silent Phone
    - and Silent Text

I was skeptical of both of these until I learned that the designer was none other than Phil Zimmermann of the original PGP encryption suite. So I trust the crypto behind it. Any video or chat session can give you encrypted messages. Better still is the 'Burn Notice' function, a Silent Text feature that allows users to decide how long a message is available before deleting it from both the sending and the receiving device. According to designers at Silent Circle, the burn timer works differently for the sender and the receiver of the message:

- For the sender, the timer will start as soon as the message is sent.
    - For the person receiving the message, the timer will

start once the message as been displayed on Silent Text's conversation screen.

These are the highlights.

Unfortunately, opsec isn't a product one can buy. It's a 24/7 mindset where 90% of the reasons you'll get caught have more to do with your offline self than anything you do online. Most newcomers to the philosophy of opsec aren't able to do this because we humans are wired to trust rather than doubt.

BLACKPHONE 2

II. Blackphone 2

Far from being a 'burner' phone that you'd toss away, the Blackphone's successor just may be the most unhackable smartphone to ever come along. But unhackable to whom?

That's the million dollar question you need to answer before you plop down over $700 bucks for one. Are you a secret agent? Double agent? Hacker? NSA escapee? Or are you just a businessman on his way to China who needs something hack-proof?

Right out of the gate you'll notice it's based around a Google operating system. You're shaking your head, I know. So was I. Avoid Google. Full stop. Go with something like Gentoo Linux with SELinux if you want a secure smartphone. And you're right. If you need serious security to avoid any state surveillance, that's the golden route. In fact if you've got an alphabet agency after you, don't use a smartphone at all. But for everyone else out there whose last name isn't Snowden, read on.

The phone itself is a miniature version of the black slab in 2001: A Space Odyssey, the one that killed the entire team. Monolithic and eerie looking, the specs are a decent upgrade from it's younger brother, but as we'll see the real meat and potatoes is the ease of use it gives you.

Display Screen: 5.5inches, 1080p LCD
   CPU: octacore Qualcomm Snapdragon 615
   RAM: 3GB
   Storage: 32GB; microSD slot
   Operating system: Silent OS 2 built on Android 5.1.1
   Camera: 13MP rear camera, 5MP front-facing camera
   Connectivity: LTE, Wi-Fi, Bluetooth and GPS
   Dimensions: 152 x 76 x 7.9mm
   Weight: 165g

The Good:
   Multitasking: A dream! The Snapdragon 615 handled everything I threw at it except for games, and there's little sense in those since that's not what you're buying the device for.

Charge: Lasted me almost a full day, but the way I bounce around apps drained a lot of juice from the device, so I had to use it sparingly to not have to charge it every day.

Useability: There was little visual difference from stock Android, with no penalties in the Google Play Store. What's available on my Samsung Galaxy Tab 4 is available here.

Security: The Stock Android appearance is misleading. There's tons of security settings under the hood for you though. You don't even need the Security Center app to hold your hand either (though you can if you want). You can set any app to only have access to location data, the web, or nothing. Up to you.

It reminded me a lot of the Cyanogen OS, which I highly recommend if you're unfamiliar with it. A few of the goodies are as follows:

- Define 'spaces' where Google cannot tread. Within this space, it is 'jailed' in a sense, and one space cannot share data with another. I had one for my contacts, work data, writing docs, taxes and email, with each being in their own 'space' and not able to reach over the fence, so to speak.

- Manage which apps live in each space.

- Quarantine any app if you only want to test drive it. That way if a catastrophe ensues, the damage is contained. Think of what the bomb disposal guys do with the bomb. Similar effect of running a suspicious app in a VM (virtual machine).

- Security updates are quick and easy to install.

- Though pricey, you pay for the software's development and ecosystem which fuel the many features it has. Sure, an iPhone is a snuggier fit for the average Joe than this phone, and as the hardware is faster and sleeker, it's easy to learn, annnnd access to the iOS system is unmatched.

- But then the Blackphone never claims to take the place of the iPhone for end users anyway, and it's not a patch on the Blackphone if what you really need is security or anonymity.

- According to Silent Circle they had a high level of cooperation from Qualcomm, and are working on having a fully audited baseband. But for now they treat baseband as a hostile router and encrypt Silent Phone voice, video and text before it goes out over radio.

The Bad:

- WiFi: 4G speeds were better than I expected, but the WiFi was laggy. On some days it was more laggy than others. It wasn't as bad what you'd get in Manila but considering the price I expected better. Not a deal breaker though.

- Encrypted messages & calls are only for Silent Phone users, though you can call others who don't own a Blackphone. Just not encrypted calls.

- Rear camera (13-megapixel) shoots dull indoor pictures. Outdoors is much better.

- Price is $799 (US). If you're not the privacy-minded type, you'll likely buy something else.

- If 'Google' is on the front screen, it's usually a red flag.

Now for The Ugly

Having lived in Niagara Falls I could write a book on my encounters with Toronto police and how invasive and downright horrifying it can be to get a snarky one on a rainy day, double that for a border officer. That snarkiness gets worse if you get sent to secondary inspection. The kicker is that this is just the phone to get you there all the quicker if you take the bait they'll drop - which they always do.

Visually, it's a remarkable little security device. You can bet the ranch they'll make a remark or two about this little black beauty as merely possessing it may ruffle a few of their federal feathers the wrong way.

Investigation going on? You'll experience heightened scrutiny. What're you hiding? Border guards on terrorist alert? Shakedown time. I see cars turned inside out as I drive into Buffalo, NY from Canada all the time, though I see many more if it's a national holiday.

If I were driving into Canada, Mexico or Europe, I'd stick the Blackphone in the most innocent, ridiculous looking Hello Kitty phone covering that I could lay my hands on, or even put it's electronic innards into a rival phone's chassis so as to look as boring as possible to any border guard. These guys put up with a lot of juvenile acts every day and the last thing you want is to whip out a pricey, hardened, hackle-raising security phone if you need to be low-profile.

They *want* to see a phone like this. It makes the hot summer day all the more bearable.

BOEING'S 'BLACK' PHONE OF SELF-DESTRUCTION

III. Boeing's 'Black' Phone of Self-Destruction

Before you whip out your wallet, know that this phone cannot be purchased by end users like you and I. But if you're an employee with security clearance, that means you've already consented to have any online actions monitored anyway so it's likely game over before you even fire up this baby.

The insides are nothing special: a 1.2 Ghz Cortex CPU, a 4.3 screen and average 1590 battery. What's unusual is the 'trusted module' satellite-uplink ability along with hardware-designed storage for encrypted data. It's pretty neat if you can get it but becomes outdated rather quickly.

Then there's the 'Pure Secure' security design by Boeing which resists all forms of spoofing or modding - which means no root access. So much for making it non-trackable to the NSA.

The specs may seem lacking but for a government employee there's probably acceptable specs for whatever the government wants him to do. For all we know they won't come in contact with the internet at all. Maybe email and productive apps like databases and NSA slideshows. Who knows.

Side note: At the other end is the transparency for a big name corporation. Take a company like Lockheed. Now think of an outfit like Northrup Grumman, a leading global security company that provides products in unmanned systems, cybersecurity, C4ISR, and other slick services.

Would it be a terrible thing for an intelligence agency to intercept some lackey at Northrup who conspired with a Lockheed employee to send a text to the Peruvian embassy? Maybe he offered to exchange some interesting maps for the secret of ceviche? Well maybe he did. Maybe he didn't.

Nonetheless, whenever you get a phone this specialized, it's almost always used for other big hardware that no one else has. If it's stolen, most of the time they can't use it.

But I thought you should know of it in case you're wandering around the Boeing plant one day and happen to see some fuzzy-mustached manager named Bucky Goldstein yakking into one of these. Know that he's got a good piece of tech in his hands that he's not likely to loan out - but no way is he evading his Big Brother the NSA.

BLACKBERRY

BlackBerry made headlines last year when it acquired Secusmar, the German-based voice-data encryption company with a penchant for waging war against well-funded eavesdroppers like the NSA. Prior to the acquisition, they'd worked together to pad BlackBerry devices with high security for a few high-profile politicians, one of which was Angela Merkel.

Yep, that Angela Merkel, Chancellor of Germany. The same Merkel that the NSA spied on and who later rightly told Obama off by phone, BlackBerry to BlackBerry.

Notifications: Android has a far better notification system than other devices. Anonymity programs like Orbot and pretty much any security app rely on notifications for mission-critical network issues.

Keyboard: Hands down, Blackberry offers the best typing experience on the market. They are at the top of a very short list of makers who design physical-keyboard phones these days. In fact I've noticed my words-per-minute increased quite drastically the more I used it. This may be insignificant in a dangerous country like Iran or Zamboanga, Philippines, but while most average Joes want some level of security on their phone, it usually comes second to features and usability.

Future Customers & Support: After spending a month researching the BlackBerry market I can tell you that I was taken aback when I discovered how much they've cut back on marketing and administration. They dropped from almost $400 million to $200 million. People who don't follow markets might think that's par for the course, but it isn't. That's big bucks. Huge bucks. In fact it's almost as if BlackBerry doesn't want to grow. And they *need* to grow but with these kind of budget slashes it's unlikely many new customers will be forthcoming in future years.

So what does this mean for security?

It means patches to exploits and security holes will be filled sparingly, if at all. A bad thing. The silver lining is that, much like a few non-Windows systems, BlackBerry may simply cease to be interesting to most hackers out there. There simply won't be enough people using them to justify exploits or hacktivism or extortion-by-virus dry runs. But that isn't nearly enough to make up for the bad.

There's also the fact that much of the top sales come from South Africa. For the record I don't think that it's CIA operatives either. More than likely it's teenagers being able to talk incognito without fear of the parents butting into their business. Teenagers who'd rather use a *physical keyboard* than a touch screen. Teenagers that use BB7 phones rather than the BB10s. The handwriting on the wall seems to be that within 5 years we'll see BlackBerry folding up the big tent and heading elsewhere.

As to Blackberry's security abilities in the here and now, read on to the next section.

BLACKBERRY SECURITY

If you're an Android user you may wonder just how secure BlackBerry really is. What makes the network itself more secure than Android?

Well the truth of it is that security is tough to implement and *tougher* to stay on top of. The king of the fortress must protect every entry point in the entire estate, while any foreign invader only needs <u>one vulnerability to exploit</u>. That's because they only have to get lucky once. Security even on BlackBerry is only as strong as its weakest link. That's *you*, my friend.

It's not entirely different than electricity or a home invader, for both follow the path of least resistance. But if you lock down your fortress with airtight security and fill your moat to the brim with piranha yet forget about the secret entrance leading up from the sewers, well there goes your security plan. Right out the window. The best guard in the world can't defend against an arrow to the back of the neck.

To it's credit, BlackBerry has something called <u>COPE</u>, which stands for Company Owned Personally Enabled Devices. You can read why this is good security elsewhere but suffice it to say its what your security needs are that counts.

A friend of mine in Korea says he as well as his family all receive malware-phishing texts on a daily basis. Usually they're the kind with fake links, but look like the genuine article. If you click on the link using an Android phone, your screen gets sent to the thief. Now he can see it all. He says this is a widespread problem in South Korea, but only on Android phones. Not so in a BlackBerry.

JAILBROKEN PHONES

One of the biggest differences between Android, iPhone and BlackBerry is that BlackBerry is designed with good security from the first layer on up *at the hardware level.* For many others such hardened security begins at the app level - the surface of an operating system. If you jailbreak your phone then that trust-module is broken and any hacker worth his salt can, on his worst day, grab data housed between the operating system level and the application level *but only if you don't take steps to secure it yourself.*

That's the tradeoff with a jailbroken phone. You get more flexibility and convenience but at the cost of security. It works the other way around, too. With more security comes less flexibility. Take your BBM messages, for instance. It's very difficult, unlike on Android, for contacts such as those in an address book to be sent elsewhere without your approval. You're the one in charge of who you converse with. Deny them or accept them. Can you deny the government?

Yes, you can, by using whatever standard of encryption you desire on a BES server. That said, you can be compelled by a judge to fork over your password as is the case with many who were arrested for tax evasion. The way around this is to never allow your IP address or *any other identifying information* about you to find its way into the hands of an adversary. And these days, learning how to hide your IP address is the kindergarten equivalent of learning the alphabet.

ENCRYPTING FILES ON BLACKBERRY

There exists several different encryption apps you can use on BlackBerry for anonymous messaging. My personal favorite is PGP, but then its an app that's had over a decade of development. Thought it works beautifully on Black-Berry, there may come a day when you simply want to encrypt files natively without the help of any third party apps. Here's how:

- From your home screen, swipe down
    - Choose settings, security and privacy - encryption
    - From here you can choose any of these:
    Set Device-Encryption to On
    Set Media Card Encryption to On
    Set your device's password (required)

You will find that it's not possible to select files/folders by themselves to encrypt but rather the entire device/media card.

DECRYPTING FILES

Choose Settings, then Encryption
    Move slider to Media or Device from On to Off
    Enter the password you set previously

<u>Important</u>: Know that implementing the above gives you an encryption key native to your phone so that if you erase this device then the key *gets erased as well*. If that happens, any data that was on this device is unaccessible without that key. To put this in perspective, if you lose your BlackBerry but still retain your microSD card that has your encrypted files (encrypted by the system that is now in the hands of someone else), you **cannot** get your files on the microSD back either, even if you use a new BlackBerry. This is linked to the system password on the device itself.

The following apps come highly recommended should you need a third-party app that encrypts individual files:

                      Hide My Pics
                      Titan Files

Max Hide & Encrypt
Secret Keeper

One thing to note is that when you encrypt your entire device, any caller's name won't appear once the device goes into a locked state. You'll see their number but not their identity. The reason for this is because the device memory becomes partially-encrypted with each instance of unlocking the device. Some users choose to encrypt only the microSD card for this very reason.

Once again, let me restate that wiping your device will render the microSD card <u>UNRECOVERABLE</u> unless it is decrypted first. The password is only used to encrypt the key, and the key is randomly generated. This is why the entire device doesn't have to be re-encrypted when you change your password.

DISABLE AUTO UPDATES

If there is one thing I've always hated about operating systems out of the box, it's automatic updates. I *loathe* them. Android is notorious for this and it was the first thing I changed when buying a Samsung Galaxy tablet a few years back.

BlackBerry isn't much different and many encryption users simply don't like auto-updates since they tend to break personalized settings and heaven only knows what else. Where security is concerned, you want full control over your device since one update can destroy your anonymity.

Often whenever a new update is released, if the device is WiFi-connected the update is downloaded in the background and installed automatically. Then the user is suddenly asked to restart. Not good.

He could be in an important business meeting in the middle of a presentation when this happens. Or on a stakeout and get the update just when the crap is about to hit the fan. Not fun for a device that brags about being the best around at security when it never *asks* you for permission to start with.

So here's how we turn it off:
   - Choose Settings, then Software Updates. Look towards the bottom of the Updates page and choose Options.

- In the Options page, the slider is present to Enable/Disable Updates. Choose according to your needs.

GENERIC BURNERS

Older & Generic Burner Phones (aka Cheap Phones)

Need an emergency phone? Then you don't need an expensive Blackphone. Give the TracFone a spin. They own Net10 & StraightTalk, both prepaid carriers, and make a few 'bare bones' phones that'll do the job just fine. The trade off is limited support. We'll discuss those at length along with a few phones I've used that aren't really phones at all. That means no GPS, 3G or even LTE. But you get a much longer-lasting battery. There's pros and cons to every one of them.

If on the other hand you need something for *'special'* emergencies, then GPS is the last thing you want. Here's why.

Let's say a cell tower pings your burner phone's location every 15 minutes or so, then saves the geolocation data and time stamp. A determined adversary might be able to query events where phone A (your super secret prepaid phone) was within 30 feet of a not-so-secret phone B for 6 hours or so, with work/driving time factored into it too. How do we prevent this from happening?

The simple way is to never leave Phone A powered on anywhere near your real-identity phone (phone B). In fact secret phone A should always, without question, remain stored at a distant location even if it's in a storage unit with your real name front and center.

As long as the battery's taken out.

This battery only gets removed if you need to 'go dark'. That's when the real phone is far away from you and believe me there's far less risk this way. If you neglect to do this, an adversary with sufficient resources (pretty much anyone with a shiny badge these days) can pinpoint both signals and correlate them to your real identity.

At any rate, as we go through these cheap phones, remember what your security needs are and that no amount of cash is too much for good security. You get what you pay for in this life, and good lawyers are more expensive that good phones and good opsec.

NOKIA LUMIA 520

This phone makes a great burner phone as it's so cheap. Being a Windows phone, you'll have to tweak it to whatever anonymity services you require. Add to that there's a mile-long list at the end in the next section where I cover anonymity apps. The bonus is that it's a steal at under $50 bucks most places. When searching for a phone, I typically read the 1-star reviews first to gauge whether it's a deal killer or not. Now for the stats.

Cons - Not all that glitters is gold. In other words, don't expect the gold standard for such a small price. This phone is lousy for hikers on the Appalachian trail in need of good GPS, but for cloak and dagger purposes it fits the bill nicely.

Odd Camera - Flash is non-existent and there's no front camera either. Photo quality is also quite poor for those photographer-tourists who always seem to wander into North Korea.

Limited Customization - The 520 doesn't sport too much in the way of separate profiles with different settings. I like to keep my work profile separate from my home profile, with each having a distinct ring tone (my ghost phone has no volume setting). The volume settings on the Lumia refused to allow me to make the two distinct. Mind you it *does* offer volume, just not for many profiles.

<u>App Inferiority</u> - You get what you pay for. The many apps for the Lumia 520 are quite humble next to what's offered for Android. And that's the silver lining. Modern, whiz-bang apps found on Android often have trackers that are difficult to disable and like to 'phone home' far too often for my liking.

<u>Moto G</u> - Prepaid Version

Another great burner phone. It uses Android and comes at under $100.

Specs:

4.5 inch 720p HD TFT display

Quad-core 1.2GHz processor with 450MHz

UMTS HSPA+, CDMA EVDO Rev A

5MP rear camera, plus front facing camera, 8GB Internal Memory

This is <u>the one</u> you want if your on a budget. When I first test drove this I wanted to see if I could use it as a WiFi mini-tablet. I skipped activation and ended up giving them no info at all and it's worked fine ever since. Just swipe off-screen and go into options, then turn airplane mode on. After doing this it didn't access any mobile network and never prompted me at all, so I just set wifi to on or off manually.

It's a nice little mini tablet. Good for privacy. Security? You can do better, and a Samsung Galaxy Tab she ain't. But it has decent resolution and can be used with Flixter, Google Play and even games. You'll get two free texts with Verizon so you'll know if it's working or not.

MOTOROLA EX-431G

The next excellent burner is the Motorola EX-431G, a TracFone that comes with a keyboard and triple-plus minutes for life. The price varies between twenty and forty dollars and like before, you get what you pay for. This is a feature phone and not an Android phone. That means no unlimited talk, text and internet, so if you want a plan like that then you'll need to use their sister company, Straight-Talk. The stats are as follows:

Full QWERTY Keyboard
    Double/Triple Minutes (depends on model)
    2MP Camera
    MP3 Player
    MicroSD Card (up to 32GB)
    Mobile Web
    Bluetooth
    Hands-Free Speaker
    FM Radio
    500 Entry Phone Book

Voicemail, Caller ID, Call Waiting, Alarm Clock

MOTOROLA MOTO G (3RD GENERATION)

A bit expensive for a burner phone, but at $179, I peg this little phone mainly for those needing sanity over anonymity, like parents with kids since it's waterproof, but can also be great for grandmas, bathrooms with soapy floors and cars in need of better communications. It's not for special ops or survival scenarios.

Specs:

- Advanced water resistance
- 13 MP camera which includes a color-balancing dual LED Flash
- 5" HD display; Brilliant display quality and the strength of Corning
- Gorilla Glass
- Quad core processing power in a great value product
- 5MP rear camera with a VGA front facing camera
- 24hr battery performance with a 2470mAh battery

- Expandable memory; Slot for an microSD card with 32 GB capacity.
- 4G LTE Speed; Browse, stream music, watch video, and play games at blazing speed.

The display isn't the best and 1GB is pretty minimal but it handles like a much more expensive device and as expected Android didn't cough up any problems. The camera too plays nice with the owner and since it ships with IPX7 - which allows for half an hour submersion in water w/no damage - you could do a lot worse. One major con though is that the battery is NOT removable. Remember what we said about the NSA being able to track phones with the battery still inside.

MOTOROLA I355

This is the survivalist's dream phone. It's cheap at around $15 at most places like ebay, and fast. It also supports Direct Talk. Direct Talk in case your're wondering is when a phone has the ability (like many Nextel phones) to grant 2-way radio chat, effectively *bypassing the cell towers*. It needs a sim card to be able to do this, but the sim card doesn't actually connect to a network/tower.

The older DirectConnect involved two phones connecting to a cell tower and from there all messages were relayed to wherever. But Direct Talk bypasses cell towers completely. This came about because many Nextel customers found their jobs bringing them to areas that required walkie-talkies. This solved that problem nicely.

Points to Note

The range varies but 3 miles out is not uncommon. Believe it or not, having a good antenna (that is, extending it) helps this range considerably.

- Incognito one-on-one calls are supported, even group calls. You can even have twenty users participate in a group call if their close enough. This is ideal for everyone but hunters since the 'blip' sound is fairly loud.

- The i355 was once one of Nextel's babies on the iDen network (now defunct and why they're so darned cheap now). To use a sim from a different network you must have an unlock code which is about twenty bucks or so from an online 'unlock shop'.

This isn't to say the i355 is the only DirectTalk phone. There are others that support it, mostly Nextel phones.

Nextel ic402
    Nextel ic502
    Nextel ic602
    Nextel ic902
    Nextel i275
    Nextel i315
    Nextel i325
    Nextel i335
    Nextel i355
    Nextel i365
    Nextel i425
    Nextel i455
    Nextel i560
    Nextel i570
    Nextel i580
    Nextel i615
    Nextel i670

Nextel i760
Nextel i776
Nextel i850
Nextel i870
Nextel i880

TRACFONE

Samsung S150G (TracFone)

Next up is the Samsung S150G, also a TracFone. Some phones advertised as 'Prepaid' aren't so cheap. The price sometimes doesn't justify what you get as you don't need to spend $50 dollars for a burner phone. This Tracphone though can be had for as little as $10 bucks. Not quite the i355, but then few are.

On the Samsung SGH-S150G you'll find a large keypad with large buttons that make dialing numbers and typing text messages easy. And that's a lifesaver in a hard storm with 50MPH winds. The specs are as follows:

TracFone Double Minutes features an LCD color display
    Auto redial
    Keypad lock
    Alarm clock
    Phonebook with up to 1,000 entries

Polyphonic ringtones
Talk Time: up to 15 hours
Standby Time: 10.4 days
Includes battery, charger, activation card and services guide

DISASTER PREPAREDNESS

I bought one of the aforementioned pre-paid phones in 2015 in Ontario, Canada with cash just to see if I could be truly anonymous in doing so. Wal-Mart was the buying place and I knew there'd be security cam footage that could identify me as the buyer, both in the store, in the parking lot and on the streetlight cams.

If I'd wanted to I could've rigged a fairly good disguise that'd throw off a decent investigator I suppose but I wasn't engaged in anything shady so I just waltzed in like a wino off the street. When I activated it at a nearby college, something struck me as it began to rain.

These types of phones are ideal for being disaster-prepared as the charge outlasts fully-fledged smartphones and tablets by a country mile. If you want some extra insurance you could even buy a couple of additional $10 phones to get the extra batteries (what they'd cost on most sites anyway).

In a looting and flood situation where you've got gangs roaming the streets and breaking into BestBuy to steal LCD TVs (a la Katrina), these simple cheap burners could be lifesavers for your entire family. Better yet, several families joined at the hip and coordinating security and ration procedures might save everyone involved from ending up like those poor Joes stranded at the New Orleans Superdome during Hurricane Katrina.

Another reason to have several is the FCC. They require that all cell phones must have 911-call ability even if you're not with any carrier. For this reason I rarely throw out my old devices. Many can still dial 911, with the Emergency Dialer usually located at the bottom of the locked phone.

Points to Note

- You may find yourself stranded in a hurricane. Or a civil war. Voice may be down, so you need to learn how to text or get a UHF & GMRS radio to contact family and loved ones. Cell phone companies usually install just enough equipment to handle normal peak usage. So if a large number of people all try to talk at once it can cause a lot of issues even when everything is working optimally.
- When the Cincinnati bridge collapsed in 2007, cell users could only initially call for help. After a few minutes cell phone voice calls were either too congested or blocked for use by emergency personnel. However, text messaging still worked, even though there were some delays.
- Data travels on a different network than voice calls and because of its nature, can be retransmitted by the network until it finally reaches your phone. So, even in the event of a brief data interruption, the network will

continually try to send your text messages until they reach your cell phone.

This makes it ideal for emergency notification, especially in the initial stages of an emergency.

If you are trying to get a message to a group of people, set up a group email list on your email service so you can broadcast instructions.

Yes, I realize that your internet service might be down but you could even set this up on your email service right on your cell. Also realize that nearly ALL cell phones now have a way to receive a text message unless they are over 10 years old. Yep, a lot of people think they don't have that service, but they do. There are limitations on some of the cell phones in getting messages of course. Some are limited to about 100 characters so if you're sending a broadcast, you'll want it to be short and precise.

Anyway, you can build all sorts of scenarios as well as your own color alert system to help get the message out in a short number of characters.

Personal Note

In 2015 I decided to buy a handful of these cheap prepaid phones, only I swore to myself I'd keep them activated in case something Really Bad happened (which later did) and I needed something other than my usual cell phone. I found that if you add twenty bucks or so to them every few months, they'll stay active and give you a nice stack of 'emergency' minutes as long as you don't go hog wild with talk time. I keep one in every vehicle as well as a charger in case I'm on a trip without my cell. For strict anonymity though this comes up a bit inadequate. But it will give you a line of communication with the wife, kids or other family members who you may need to call in dire situations.

Each of these phones is connected to a different carrier's network, like Sprint and Verizon, in case one of them goes down in an Armageddon-like scenario. As stated before, these prepaid phones have amazingly more battery-charge (and can withstand drops/spills) than your average smartphone.

Craigslist

The value of Craigslist is heavily dependent on your region, but some very nice phones can be acquired using it.

One thing though. Always *always* carry a burner when you deal with anyone on Craigslist and especially when buying expensive items like gaming laptops, cars or rare firearms.

Come armed if you can. Let a friend know where you're going. Not that you're doing anything shady, but you've no idea if you're meeting the next Evil Dead fan who wants to pick up where the cabin demons left off. The level of evil out there is escalating. You want to leave as few digital breadcrumbs as possible. Never let strangers know you've got a nice gun filled basement with a safe full of cash and i355 phones.

National Guard Sergeant Jim Vester from Indianapolis was killed while trying to complete a Craigslist transaction for an iPad. It was a setup from the start over what amounted to $400. Such a tragedy may have been averted if he'd arranged to meet in a public place for the transaction. Sadly, he did not.

If you must use this service however, when posting the

ad, do not allow email contact. Just put your contact info in the ad body itself. i.e. the phone number and specify *calls only*. This eliminates scams and weeds out the not so serious buyers as well as stupid "Is the BBQ pit in the background for sale?" and "what lowest price take for?" emails.

Scams

And beware of the Paypal/eBay/Craigslist scam. It goes like this. They send you a fake email that looks like a PayPal email would. You then click the link in said email, which then directs you to a website that looks *exactly* like PayPal, only it isn't actually PayPal. You enter your username/password in said website and viola, they now have your login info.

This scam has been around for years. A safer bet is to stick with thrift stores and yard sales. Burners are one thing but for selling weapons and related stuff, you're probably better off using Armslist.com.

There's another scam, too. Avoid any craigslist buyer/seller of costly items that cannot meet you face to face. I've met dozens of scammers buying and selling fast cars and other expensive items. Only deal with locals who have cash in their hands, ready to buy.

In God we trust, all others pay cash.

QUESTIONS AND ANSWERS

Where to get the best burner phones?

If you need traceless burners, anywhere you don't usually shop that doesn't have cameras is probably a good idea. That means not in your hometown. Forget the usual shop places.

Burners are cheap with a few being only ten dollars or so, but if you're the truly paranoid type you can buy one from a different mom and pop store every time you need one, use it once for whatever security operation you need, then wipe the device and disperse the pieces in multiple locations.

Flea Markets are a good secondary source for burners. I've bought a few and they're 'just as good' as the Big Box store kind with the only caution being you need to ensure it isn't tracking you from the outset. You'll need new a SIM card as well. Failing that, there's also a few sources on the Deep Web, aka the Darknet, using Tor and Bitcoins to purchase one.

If I can't store it at my house or my office then where am I supposed to keep it? A safety deposit box?

No. In fact, never store it at a bank at all or any place secured with your ID. Store it at a friend's house instead. Oh but he doesn't want it there either because if he's your friend he probably knows all about your top secret operation and doesn't want the liability. Do you have a secure HQ set up? Somewhere private and away from cell towers where members meet? One possibility is storing it at an abandoned site, possibly in a rural setting.

What about batteries?

Batteries are a problem but not if you don't activate the phone prematurely. One solution is to keep them somewhere safe until the day you need it. Store in a PVC tube and hide in a tree with tree bark super-glued to it. If you live near a lake you'll see many places where one could be stored under a pier in a waterproof bag. Of course, you don't want to store *everyone's* batteries or phones there.

Good opsec is *hard work*.

FARADAY CAGES

A faraday bag or 'cage' is a storage place where radio waves are forbidden and by extension data, since data uses radio waves to relay messages. A nice place to hide a phone, though I can't think of even one home appliance that lends itself to simple modification for an effective Faraday cage. Microwave ovens make for one unreliable cage, believe me. Just put a burner inside and try calling it to see for yourself.

The holes are the problem. They're tiny enough to prevent the wavelengths that the microwave uses from passing through. Shorter wavelengths though (ones with more energy) *will* pass through. My twelve-year-old nephew once came over and asked what I was doing. I told him flat out then looked at him. This blank expression came along his face.

I hadn't seen him in a good long while so I showed him the same phone I saved from 1983, the same year Return of the Jedi came out. His eyes lit up.

"Wow,' he says. "I bet it's got all kinds of illegal parts," only then he grabs it and starts mashing the holes like they were smartphone buttons. He'd never seen one that required 'dialing'.

Moving on.

You'll have to buy a radio frequency shielding bag that blocks every signal to and from the cell phone, or go to PrivacyCase.com and get one from the pros. They're asking more than everyone else, but their product works quite well. They had it lab tested and the thing doesn't leak, period. No cellular, no wi-fi, no GPS, nothing.

Another option is if you own a gun cabinet made of metal. Line the inside with a 1/4' wire mesh and tin foil. Secure the tinfoil with foil duct tape. Now you can store your emergency electronics/burners with your weapons, though admittedly this is time-consuming. There's something else you outta know, too.

That cell you're carrying is constantly being tracked by this cell tower or that tower even when you turn the GPS function off. Whenever your phone breaks contact with these towers, it'll increase power to the transmitter to reestablish a connection. Power consumption goes UP and drains the battery.

Then there's the digital footprint of your cell going off the grid and then popping up somewhere else. Maybe even data related to *why* it went down. Certainly *where* it went down.

Then Barney the bored TSA guy wants to know what the deal is. He's in the airport and thinks he's Michael Weston before he got 'burned' by the CIA. He'll say, "Well lookie here, some taffer tryin' to get all stealthy. We'll teach 'em to mess with us!" Then you've got problems.

What about hiding phones in a fridge?

Edward Snowden suggested using a fridge as a kind of faraday cage. True, a few may block sound, but that has no bearing on a radio's frequency. In some models the seal-gap can even act as a rudimentary antenna! Microwave ovens aren't the solution either since the door seal blocks RF only at 2.4 ghz - which is not a cell band.

It's hard work and hard to maintain. If you slip up with any of the above, you best consider your opsec broken. Once broken it *cannot be unbroken*. It cannot be repaired since you don't know how many now know your identity. All numbers, accents, purchases, addresses and trails are now linked to you and you cannot unlink them.

It's why CIA agents work so hard at keeping a low profile. They offer verifiable (false) data that deceives outsiders into thinking something exists when it really doesn't. Unfortunately many of them lose friends and family over it, so they end up in a 'bubble' that's very hard to break out of. It's like that Eagles song: "You can check in but you can never leave."

Earlier I mentioned that your greatest weakness is yourself. There's another side to that coin and it's this: the NSA's greatest weakness is itself. They tend to rely on signal intelligence for everything at the expense of everything else. They rely too much on technology with not enough eyes on the ground. This is in your favor because they can only see what you give them, like using your burner to call your girlfriend after all mission burners have been activated.

It's an elaborate chess match of move, countermove, attack, but if you prevent them from getting near your queen, they cannot say *checkmate*.

Let me repeat it. Good opsec is hard work!

20 GHOST APPS FOR SMARTPHONES

Call me paranoid, but I've never trusted Android to completely remove *everything* an app may leave inside my phone. The uninstall process seems a little 'off' to me, as though something rotten has been left to fester underneath. Microsoft Windows is a little better, but with Android there's always some cryptic legalese about painless network access and maybe what it intends to modify, only it's in a kind of gnarled and twisted doubles-peak that even I can't untangle. Or maybe I just suck at legalese.

NEVERTHELESS, a research paper came out last year that shed a lot of light on the subject of just what goes on under Android's hood. They called it Taming the Android AppStore: Lightweight Characterization of Android Apps. Here's what they did.

. . .

THEY TESTED over 2000 of the Play Store's free apps in every category using a Samsung-Galaxy S3 phone with Android 4.1. They accomplished this using a VPN which dumped IP addresses and other data using TCPdump - which monitored every app on the phone. The result wasn't pretty.

THEY FOUND that many Android apps connected (without permission) to at least one of five hundred unique websites without leaving a trail. That's right. No popups. No emails. No opt-out. It connected to all sorts of things that kill anonymity outright to say nothing about general privacy.

AD TRACKERS. Behavior analytics. Click trackers. Tracking servers. The whole anti-privacy enchilada with Google sitting fat and happy at the top of the heap with that crooked Joker's grin. So why did they not engage in a little *transparency*?

My theory is that it isn't that they don't have this ability from a technical standpoint. They do indeed. It's that they need to grant the application developer access to your private data on a consistent day-to-day basis.

SPEAKING OF PRIVATE DATA, I've found most privacy advocates to care less about staying 'hidden' from the NSA and more about hiding from corporate entities. Bragging about that hot new IP over an open mic network like Skype is, to put it mildly, crazy business.

. . .

When you get to the point in your career when you're discussing business startups, the first line of defense should always, without exception, be privacy focused. That's because Microsoft, Apple, Google and the like care zero about protecting you. You are considered by them to be their product. Their bottom line. That includes every bit of hearsay, gossip, or stock details that zip around on Skype which, if you sign on the dotted line in their Terms of Service agreement, is fair game.

In the end, it isn't patents, copyrights, and lawsuits that shield your ideas and ventures and marketable products. It's trade secrets - and that requires you to kick their corporate noses out of your tent. And your business.

So what follows is the absolute end-all-be-all of must have addon apps that'll turn your gremlin-built Android phone into a veritable fortress of doom, from which *nothing* gets in or out without your express permission. Sort of like DungeonKeeper for mobile phones, except you call the shots.

SIGNAL FOR ANDROID

First up is Signal, the popular messenger and private calling app on the Google Play Store designed by Whisper Systems. It's the combining of two very secure encryption apps called TextSecure and RedPhone, both built by the same. Both apps began on iPhone and now have been brought over to Android. Several bonuses right off the bat jumped out at me.

- The code is open source, reviewable by experts. That's a big one.
- No ads to speak of.
- Anyone can use this to communicate instantly and privately.

The above options aren't the only ones of course. They're just the ones that jumped out at *me* for *my* security needs. Yours may be different. Initially I was worried about the authorities mandating a 'back door' but then I realized that using plain old run-of-the-mill SMS is almost always intercepted by local sheriffs and municipal police to begin with. Everywhere.

Between using SMS and an open-source app by one of the most respected security researchers in the world, you probably know which one to use. My skills aren't really up to tracking the changelog on GitHub and recompiling it myself for Verizon's SMS, so I'll just trust WhisperSystems instead.

Just so you know, as soon as Microsoft paid 8.5 billion for Skype, it found itself in a much deeper U.S. jurisdiction than Windows settled for. Skype makes voice calls to the PSTN (i.e. the public switched telephone network) and when that happened, it fell under the CALEA Act. That's the Communications Assistance for Law Enforcement Act, an act initiated by the US Congress to facilitate wiretapping of U.S. domestic telephone and Internet traffic.

Skype encryption is not end to end.

And now that Microsoft lives smack dab in the middle of every conversation uttered over Skype in the USA (and even abroad), they have a nice intercept point to eavesdrop from their servers. By contrast, TextSecure (now Signal) does not own a voice service. So there's no intercept requirements. If TextSecure were ever to resort back to SMS, then law enforcement can sniff the ciphertext. But without the key, its pretty useless.

ORWEB

Orweb is a web browser created with your privacy in mind. It's newbie-friendly and, when coupled with Orbot, can shield you from network analysis, supercookies and all without running Flash, the same Flash that can introduce exploits into your Android system.

It does this by routing your traffic through international computers remotely rather than going directly into a VPN or other proxy service. It's slower this way, but ensures a level of security above that of the average user.

The problem is that it's now outdated. Obsolete. As of 2016 it has been upgraded to Orfox status. As for the old version (i.e. Orweb), the developers had this to say:

"Orweb is built upon the bundled WebView (Webkit) browser component inside of the Android operating system. This has proven to be problematic because we cannot control the version of that component, and cannot upgrade it directly when bugs are found. In addition, Google has made it very difficult to effectively control the network proxy settings of all aspects of this component, making it difficult to guarantee that traffic will not leak on all devices and OS versions."

ORFOX: TOR BROWSER FOR ANDROID

Designed with source code from Tor Browser, a few enhancements have been added to make it a rock-solid browser for Android. With NoScript, HTTPS Everywhere and Tor Browser Button added in, it's a rock-solid tool for anonymous browsing.

Differences to note:

1.) Other than the fact Orweb is outdated, Orfox is vastly superior to Orweb as Orweb focuses on minimal browser-fingerprinting and cookies with fewer writes to disk.

2.) Orweb takes up less than 2MB. Orfox comes in at 27MB. This is mainly due to Orfox becoming a more robust browser with a longer feature set.

From the Developer:

"Orfox is built from the same source code as Tor Browser (which is built upon Firefox), but with a few minor modifications to the privacy enhancing features to make them compatible with Firefox for Android and the Android operating system."

- Orfox **REQUIRES** Orbot app for Android to connect to the Tor network.

In as many ways as possible, we adhere to the design goals of Tor Browser, by supporting as much of their actual code as possible, and extending their work into the additional Android components of Firefox for Android.

The Tor software protects you by bouncing your communications around a distributed network of relays run by volunteers all around the world: it prevents somebody watching your Internet connection from learning what sites you visit, it prevents the sites you visit from learning your physical location, and it lets you access sites which are blocked."

TELEGRAM

Telegram is a message app that focuses on security. It's fast, simple and ad-free. A few of the benefits they offer are:

- <u>Cloud Storage</u>: Telegram syncs across all your devices so you can always access your data. Your message history is also stored in the Telegram cloud.

- <u>Group Chat & Sharing</u>: you can form large group chats of up to 1000 members if you need to.

- <u>Secret Chats</u>: These are messages that, according to Telegram, can be programmed to self-destruct automatically from both participating devices. This way you can send all types of disappearing content: messages, photos, videos and files. Secret Chats also use end-to-end encryption to ensure that a message can only be read by its intended recipient.

So how secure is it? That largely depends on your security needs. If you require rock-solid security like the kind political dissidents in China use, then no. There's lots of questions floating around on the lack of peer review as well. But if you only want to keep Google (or the spouse) out of your affairs, then yes.

Using an app that has end-to-end encryption is better than non end-to-end and that uses closed source (i.e. Whatsapp), with no way to peer review it. Telegram also does not store your secret chats, and the data stays encrypted until it arrives at the receiver's phone.

However, it uses non-standard crypto. Though there are those in the security community who become nervous whenever a developer does this, the bottom line is that you and you alone must determine if this app fills your anonymity needs, or whether you need some other app like CryptoCat.

CHAT SECURE

ChatSecure is an open-source chat client that supports encryption over XMPP. Previously known as 'Gibberbot', it's progressed to be a fairly reliable chat app for privacy. The downside is that it cannot stay connected or in an 'always-on' state since Apple forbids it. The upside is that it's free and works on every platform: Android, iPhone, Mac with Adium, Linux with Jitsi, and Windows with Pidgin.

<u>Features:</u>
    - Every message you send with ChatSecure is private so long as your recipient uses an OTR-compatible IM client
    - Delivers audio, photos, files and text.
    - Messages sent aren't stored in your phone's memory.
    - If used with Orbot, it can bypass many firewalls and blacklists.
    - Supports multiple accounts

K-9 AND OPENKEYCHAIN

Encrypted E-mail

K-9 Mail is built upon Android's native email application, but is open-source. It's main advantage for you is simplifying email management. If you've got multiple accounts and need encryption, K-9 is your baby since it uses OpenPGP via OpenKeychain for encrypting messages.

OpenKeychain EASYPGP integrates with K-9 and strengthens anonymous communications. The encryption it uses ensures that any communication can only be read by those with the proper key. When your recipient opens your message, they can see it is digitally signed by you (or not). In fact that's the whole point of PGP, also known as Pretty Good Privacy. For your eyes only. That's to ensure you're speaking with the right person.

You can also search for other people's keys online. Just remember that PGP is useful for two things:

1. Privacy and Security, and
2. Authenticity.

By privacy, I mean that you can prevent people from

seeing things you don't want them to see. For example, you can encrypt an email to someone or encrypt a file with a list of passwords.

By <u>authenticity</u>, I mean that you can ensure a message was sent/written by the person you think it was and that it wasn't modified by a third party. Of course, these two can be combined.

I like to remember the opening scene from Wargames, where two missile silo operators have to turn their key simultaneously before inputting the nuclear launch codes.

<u>Points to Note:</u>

Don't worry about reverting to your old email should K-9 not be to your liking. This is easily done by uninstalling or going to

Settings --> Applications --> Manage Apps -->

and choosing your app before clicking on "clear defaults". This resets the default app for that function. It's sort of like installing a new browser. Chrome over Firefox, for instance. If you uninstall Chrome, Firefox will still be there for you.

The other thing is that if you want to export the K-9 settings somewhere, you will need to reboot your phone, after which the *com.fsck.k9* directory should be accessible at the topmost level of the Android system.

KEYSYNC: SYNCING TRUSTED IDENTITIES

KeySync allows you to sync identities between OpenPGP and ChatSecure as well as GnuPG. The app needs to do this for purposes of establishing trust between different apps on your Android device. Trust certificates, say, for Pidgin and Adium, need to be converted to ChatSecure so that there's no conflicting identities. It's sort of like having the same name and identity that matches all your credit cards. You can use Discover and MasterCard at the same place because of the identity match. Same concept here.

Syncing to ChatSecure

Now then. Let's say you wanted to sync between ChatSecure on your phone and maybe an app on your PC or laptop. Here's what you'd have to do:

- Ensure your phone is connected via USB.

- Powerup KeySync and let it detect your system.

- If it fails to find it, it will store the *otr_keystore.ofcaes* to your phone's SD card. From there, ChatSecure can locate it.

- Within ChatSecure you can go to your Account screen & choose "Activate KeySync." Then you use the QRCode that you can see in KeySync to complete this process. And that code acts as the key/passphrase to your keystore, so don't lose it or email it to anyone. It all sounds very convoluted, but you'll see it isn't once you go through it.

LASTPASS PASSWORD MANAGER

I absolutely love what I can do with LastPass. What does it do? Well you can use LastPass to store logins, create complex passwords and keep track of any team members passwords you have to keep under lock and key. You only need to remember one password however: *your* Last-Password.

It fills in logins for you and syncs passwords & passphrases anywhere you need it. That's not all. Some other neat things you can do (though admittedly a few break your anonymity!), are:

• Save and autofill usernames/passwords for all online accounts

• Streamline online shopping with Form Fill profiles (danger Will Robinson!)

• Store memberships, credit cards, & sensitive data in Secure Notes (Risky!)

• Search for logins and notes from your vault (useful)

• Organize sites by folders (very useful)

• Enable multifactor authentication to lock down your LastPass account.

- Share logins with friends/family (This is an absolute no-no unless you want to kill your anonymity outright.)
- Audit the strength of your passwords with the LastPass Security Challenge

In light of the above you may think what's the point since several features use services that are known to be hostile to privacy. Well, you don't need to use LastPass then. Many don't for the simple reason it is web-based. Try a Keypass database instead for offline activity, or sync with Dropbox.

Actually come to think of it, that's risky too since if you're unencrypted laptop or PC gets stolen, then you must consider *all* passwords compromised.

But let's compare an offline password manager like Password Safe with an online manager like LastPass for a moment. Weight the risks, so to speak.

Believe it or not, offline password managers carry risk just like online managers. Some believe that the password 'safe' file acts as the mother of all risks since it's the bottom ace card in a house of cards. But that's true for your PC too since all it takes is one keylogger to compromise your system.

Without any manager at all a keylogger can record every pass you use. With a manager app, you can conceivably lose ALL of your passwords in one fell stroke. For this reason I suggest you pick one or the other. They both harbor strengths and weaknesses with one strength being that you can use your passwords on anyone's computer. That's pretty convenient under almost any scenario.

Alas, there's always a hacker lurking around, and make no mistake that an online database can be breached by him and him alone. In that case, everyone goes down. Tens of thousands of users just like you. In this there is the safety in numbers element unless the hacker in question decides to sell every bit of data to the highest bidder. The silver lining is that you'll know about such a breach almost immediately from your online provider (assuming the company doesn't want a class-action lawsuit.)

LINPHONE: ENCRYPTED VIDEO AND VOICE OVER IP (VOIP)

Linphone is a free voice over IP, or VoIP service, and SIP client, currently developed by Belledonne Communications in France. It's now available for AppleiOS and Android as well as PCs, with the biggest advantage being it isn't limited to voice and video. You can send texts, chat, make multiple calls and even call up your friends for an audio conference.

Three major new capabilities have been added: a text messaging feature (chat) with delivery status notification, multiple calls and audio conferencing. In addition, Linphone supports audio with speex , G711 ,ILBC, GSM, SILK, G722, OPUS, and video with the VP8 codec.

If you want to talk to your partners using Tor then you'll need to use Onioncat at both ends since Linphone uses UDP. Instructions on using Linphone for anonymous VoIP over Tor can be found at the Whonix site. Just remember that Tor adds considerable latency so it will not be like those crystal clear calls Jason Bourne gets in a firefight in some back alley in Pakistan.

OBSCURACAM: THE PRIVACY CAMERA

Like Pinta and Gimp, ObscuraCam allows you to blur faces in any photo or video that could lead to your identification. Use pixelation or blackout or even a funny nose/glasses combo to edit out your identity. The app itself is designed by the GuardianProject and Witness.org, a human rights training organization.

Unfortunately the ObscuraCam app itself does not encrypt files in transit. For that you'll have to resort to some other encryption app like PGP or Veracrypt and then go through the usual encryption routine like so:

- Install the app
   - Create an encrypted container after choosing a container size for encrypting
   - Send the file (along with the password your recipient needs via PGP). Simple.

METADATA

Put simply, metadata is used by search engines, intelligence agencies and even grocery store chains to track you. Obscuracam removes this. Things like GPS coordinates, time/date of image, phone owner's name/nic, and phone model aren't recorded. In my view this is light years better than being able to blur faces on Facebook -which you should not be on anyway if you want privacy. The Exif Data Firefox plugin also makes a great companion tool as it can delete metadata from jpegs. Now onto some questions.

What else does metadata cover?

In theory the amount of metadata available on a person is near infinite. But they don't have quantum computers yet which means the amount of data on any one person is limited. We aim to limit it even more since even a single file can reveal a lot about you as a person.

What kind of files contain metadata?

- Any kind. Word docs, jpegs, bitmaps, mp3s. Everything and anything that carries a digital signature or hash can tell them where you live, what you listen to, who dumped you and whether you squirt your ketchup on your fries or on the side at the In n' Out burger.

I'm a novelist. I don't care about any of that.

- Sorry to tell you this but novelists have a lot to worry about too, especially if they're self-publishers. Actually traditional pubbers too, since French writer Grégory Delacourt was sued by Scarlett Johansson for 'stealing' her image. But that's another tale.

Novelists, writers and copywriters have to worry about privacy just like Stephen King. The master of horror storytelling once revealed his biggest blunder. He was asked if there was anything in his career that he regretted doing or saying, other than writing Maximum Overdrive. He said, "That damn American Express commercial from the eighties. Once I'd done that, people all over the world knew my face."

ORBOT: PROXY WITH TOR

Orbot encrypts your internet traffic with Tor so that it cannot be traced. It does this by relaying traffic through relays around the world. No other tool does this like Tor, and makes it a useful privacy tool. Even the New York Times praised it.

"When a communication arrives from Tor, you can never know where or whom it's from."

Okay, fair enough. But you must decide which is the bigger risk: Your cell provider or Google. I'd say both carry equal risk but when you hand them your identity on a silver platter, well, they don't even need a judge to take you down. Only a thinly-veiled reproach. Of course some countries carry more risk than others when you take your threat model into account. Next question.

Is there a way to hide the fact I'm using Tor (Orbot) from my ISP?

Hiding Tor usage from your ISP provider isn't that hard. They'll know you're using Tor soon enough, just not what you're doing with it. They can also monitor you till the cows come home but have no idea what hidden services you're accessing nor do they have a clue which content you send or receive from while using Tor. It can be detected, however, from the Tor relay node via the IP addresses you connect to.

To hide Tor usage itself from them you'll need to use a Tor bridge to prevent them from seeing you are on the Tor network.

OSMAND: OFFLINE MAPS AND NAVIGATION

Osmand (OSM Automated Navigation Directions) is a navigation app used in conjunction with OpenStreetMap (OSM). It makes a stellar replacement for Google Maps, but it isn't anonymous unless you're offline the whole time. It uses maps from OpenStreetMap and can be downloaded using Tor.

Features:

- Works online (fast) or offline (no roaming charges when you are abroad)
- Turn-by-turn voice guidance (recorded and synthesized voices)
- Optional lane guidance, street name display, and estimated time of arrival
- Supports intermediate points on your itinerary
- Automatic re-routing whenever you deviate from the route
- Search for places by address, by type (e.g.: restaurant, hotel, gas station, museum), or by geographical coordinates.

One downside is that while the screenshots on the Play Store make it look simple, it's not. In fact it's fairly complex and the controls are somewhat unintuitive.

OSTEL: ENCRYPTED PHONE CALLS

Ostel is a product designed for keeping your calls private. So private in fact, that it offers end-to-end encryption at both ends. And if you believe the United States to be the only one data mining everything on the internet, I've got a friendly rattlesnake to sell you.

I've got some mixed feelings about Ostel and I'm sure you will to. To begin with you must register for an account at Ostel.co. That was the first red flag. From the dial pad I had to key in 9196 then click the green icon in the corner before I could speak. Then came the echo test which I found similar to Skype's test. All in all, its a hit and miss scenario, but I concede your luck may be better than mine. The pros are as follows:

- Supports: Android, iPhone, Mac, Win, Linux & Blackberry/Nokia
    - Integrates well with CSipSimple app for Android
    - Supports end-to-end encrypted using ZRTP & SRTP.
    - Makes for a great privacy tool

Cons:

Now for the cons.

Encrypted phones sound intriguing to just about every anonymity enthusiast out there, especially beginners. The problem? Configuring some of these apps can be like toying with a rattlesnake itself. Technical hurdle is putting it mildly indeed. Besides that, encrypted voice apps are really a hit and miss and here are a few reasons why.

Apps such as this one, based on my use of it, reveal a lot of counter-intuitive design decisions that don't mesh well with the Android interface, nor with what Android users are accustomed to. This isn't a problem for a technically minded person but beginners will have a hard time navigating around since a lot of these don't follow Android design specs.

Case in point: No activity light. Remember when almost every PC came with one so that you could see the hard drive being accessed? That's absent far too often these days. There's a few other red flags, one being the guessing game as to when the encryption actually began and when it ended.

- **Confusion.** Ostel was as different to Linphone as the sun is to the moon in the directions. I'm quite good guessing games but even I tended to wander around like I was in a fog, patting my hands like a blind person. I can imagine how confusing it would be for someone new to encrypted voice calls. In one instance I ended up making a call through my normal phone line with the dial pad. There was no indication this was taking place until I ran some tests to confirm it. Strike one.

- **Setting up an account** at Ostel.co was uninspiring, with the SIP provider not being clear on just what their definition of anonymity is, which bothered me. Throughout the process I kept thinking that newcomers will abandon ship when they realize they cannot call Skype anonymously (you need to call someone with a SIP client to ensure the call is private). That should be loud and clear on the front page.

- **Cannot call landlines** from Ostel and have it encrypted. This was a deal killer for me, but I'll waive the strike since you may not need to call them at all.

- **Metadata.** The app is bad at hiding it from others. Contacts, call history and such, seemed to be not terribly high on the app's priorities, unlike the Tor Browser Bundle. I admit that to compare Tor with encrypted phone use is perhaps premature as it *is* in it's infancy, but metadata is the hook, line and sinker of the NSA and thus must be executed as a priority one mission objective.

- **They log data.** They claim to log enough data to run the service, but it sounds like the same ploy I hear from VPN providers looking to cover their backsides. We know VPN companies are great at offering privacy but for anonymity, many come up lacking. Strike two.

- **No Tor support.** Also a deal killer, but this may be due to the prematurity of the service and not related to the company itself. Voice over IP doesn't work well with Tor anyway due to the way Tor works (torrents as well), which means Orbot won't work well with it. Strike three.

TEXTSECURE

TextSecure (now Signal) is an open-source communication app that allows you to avoid SMS fees and share media with colleagues, friends and the like, privately. We list it here if you're a little uneasy about using Signal.

So how secure is it?

Very secure, though obviously not as secure as the newly revamped Signal app. An interesting (though insanely technical) research paper is available online and is called 'How Secure is TextSecure'. It's put out by the Horst Institute for IT Security and their conclusion was that three apps outside of Tor outshine all others for anonymity: Threema, Surespot and TextSecure. You can draw your own conclusions, but I've tested every app and found TextSecure to be a great tool to use for any operation that requires staying off the grid.

PIXELKNOT: HIDDEN MESSAGES

Pixelknot allows you to send a short message within a photo that only the recipient can read. The practice involves what is known as 'steganography', or the act of embedding a hidden message in any format. In that vein it's somewhat similar to PGP, but uses the F5 algorithm to obscure your message. The developers (i.e. The Guardian Project) issued this standard to strive toward:

- Have the original image appear, to the trained human eye, unedited.

 - Have the bytes of the image appear, to a trained analyst, undistorted so much so as to arouse suspicion.

 - Have the complete message be recoverable no matter how it is transmitted.

I've used it for other types of communication but let's look at one in particular: Usenet. My favorite stomping ground since 1983.

 Let's assume for a moment you want to send an anonymous message to someone on Usenet, perhaps in one of the many Mp3 newsgroups, and let's also assume you don't want Google indexing that message for all eternity. (Well actually, they will anyway).

You'd first pull up the app, choose a picture to hide the message in, and send it using a Usenet posting app knowing that even though the picture itself is quite visible to others, what is encoded *therein* is not. In fact, they could not even tell that it is a picture manipulated by Pixelknot. It's true that Google will index this for eons, but until quantum computing becomes widespread, won't be able to decrypt it.

If on the other hand you post an encrypted message using PGP, well, it's obvious you don't want others to see it if you post it in designated *encryption* newsgroups. The same is true for the popular encryption containers like those of Truecrypt or Veracrypt. Any extension (unless you change it) often gives away the app used and by extension the intent of the sender.

GHOST APPS FOR THE BLACK MARKET

First up is GRAMS, the Darknet Search Engine

Grams's engine was designed to be used primarily for exploring the Deep Web. Announced on Reddit over a year ago, it has made some great strides in indexing things you cannot find on the regular web. But like Google in 1996, they're in a very early stage of indexing things, so it's not perfect and offers nowhere near the complexity that Google does.

It does share some of the traits of Google's algorithm though, like having a scoring system based on how long the listing has been up, how many transactions, and how many good reviews any one site has. That way you'll see the best listing first - similar to what you'd see using Google.

The Grams Infodesk can be reached at the Onion site here:

http://grams7enufi7jmdl.onion/infodesk

You will need Tor to access this onion site.

Duck Duck Go

DuckDuckGo strives to become the next great internet search engine that protects user's privacy and avoids the filter bubble of personalized search results that Google is so famous for.

The results are a compilation of about 50 sources including Yahoo! Search, BOSS, Wikipedia, Bing and its own Web crawler, the DuckDuckBot, among others. The best part is that while the regular search site is at DuckDuckGo.com, you can use the Duck onion site to perform a clearnet search, which adds yet another layer of security to your regular web usage. The link is at:

http://3g2upl4pq6kufc4m.onion/

Note: Obviously you will need to be connected to the Tor network for the above onion link to work.

Pros to Using DuckDuckGo

- In March, 2015, DuckDuckGo retrieved more than 9 million searches for the first time since she set sail. That month also saw the search engine retrieve more than 250 million searches. Where there are great numbers, there is camouflage. Plus, their competition could set new common rules for privacy among web service providers, which would include Google.

- You can always precede a search query with g! to see what Google's results would be. For instance:

"Mustangs !g" -> search for Mustangs on Google.

"Mustangs !gi" -> search for Mustangs on Google image

"Mustangs !yt" -> Youtube

"Mustangs !b" -> Bing

More here: https://duckduckgo.com/bang

- When DuckDuckGo lists results that it got from Yahoo or Bing, your phone or laptop isn't getting cookies from Yahoo or Bing.

Cons to Using DuckDuckGo

- DuckDuckGo labels itself as a privacy search engine, so it won't be terribly helpful to use it for things requiring location. A search for "air conditioners for sale in New Orleans, LA" will give you a craigslist-like site, followed by a contractor's webpage, and a link to YellowPages. The same search on google gives the names of some local and major-chain businesses who sell and install air conditioners.

And in case you're wondering if 'incognito' mode stops Google's tracking that results from your Google searches, the answer is no. A loud no with arms waving no. Only a non-tracking search engine like DuckDuckGo (that can guarantee your privacy) does that. Bing and Yahoo and Google will still record everything you do regardless of any incognito mode, as it affects the browser options and not the search engine of choice.

Another thing about our beloved Google, whose name keeps popping up like some handle-bar mustached villain in a bad play. Google knows your preferred home temperature *and* your work schedule when you're away at Six Flags *and* when you go to sleep and wake up, all thanks to the Nest Learning Thermostat. That, coupled with Google Pictures (which logs images on your phone or PC) makes for one very bright laser red dot on your back. People love convenience over security, even before Ben Franklin wrote his famous quote on liberty and security.

Google Wallet? Again, convenience. They keep all data related to every purchase you make, every sale, and coordinate it all with every email message you write. Remember what Google founder Eric Schmidt said some years ago?

"Google will soon know more about you than you know yourself!".

They now have far more data on you than the NSA does and that data is only a warrant away. Rest assured they will not offer 1/10th the privacy that DuckDuckGo does.

NOTECIPHER

NoteCipher is a simple notepad app. All notes created and stored by this app are saved fully secured using 256-bit AES encryption. They are never stored in an unencrypted state on the disk, only in memory. It was ported to Android in 2011 by the Guardian Project.

I use this app whenever I need to write text but don't want to resort to a literal notebook. It's also available via F-Droid.

APG

OpenPGP is another good privacy app for Android. It's open source and its goal is to provide a similar OpenPGP implementation as GnuPG.

If you're browsing Darknet Markets you may run across the occasional vendor whose key wont work with APG. But this is rare. In any case you can use GnuPrivacyGuard to help.

As a side note, if you're worried about the app broadcasting that you're using Apg v.1.1. whatever (yet don't want anyone knowing you use APG), you could always edit the version before sending out any message. Example: Put Version: GnuPG v2 and anyone else would assume that's the encryption program you are using.

BITCOIN WALLET

Want to have your Bitcoins always with you? Check out Bitcoin Wallet.

You pay by quickly scanning a QR-code and if you're a merchant, you'll receive payments reliably and instantly. Bitcoin Wallet is the first mobile Bitcoin app and arguably one of the most secure.

- No registration, web service or cloud needed. This wallet is de-centralized.
- Display of Bitcoin amount in BTC, mBTC and µBTC.
- Conversion to and from national currencies.
- Sending and receiving of Bitcoin via NFC, QR-codes or Bitcoin URLs.
- Address book for regularly used Bitcoin addresses.
- When you're offline, you can still pay via Bluetooth.
- System notification for received coins.
- Sweeping of paper wallets (e.g. those used for cold storage).
- App widget for Bitcoin balance.

CHATSECURE

ChatSecure is a free and open source messaging app that features OTR encryption over XMPP. You can connect to your existing accounts on Facebook or Google, create new accounts on public XMPP servers (including via Tor), or even connect to your own server for extra security.

Unlike other apps that keep you stuck in their walled garden, ChatSecure is fully interoperable with other clients that support OTR and XMPP, such as Adium, Jitsi, and more.

Strong Cryptography

ChatSecure only uses well-known open source cryptographic libraries to keep your conversations private. Other apps may make claims about "military grade" security but, without publicly auditable source code and verifiable end-to-end encryption, you cannot be 100% safe.

Some of what it offers:

- XMPP with TLS certificate pinning.
   - OTR for verifiable end-to-end encryption and forward secrecy.
   - Tor to help bypass restrictive firewalls.
   - SQLCipher to locally encrypt conversation logs.

Anonymouth

Recall earlier what we said about looking *like everyone else* when using Tor. Enter Anonymouth.

Stylometrics is the study of a person's writing 'style'. It analyzes your writing and creates a trackable profile out of it. In other words, your 'voice' in your writing or the way you phrase simple statements, word length, word choice, misspelled words and so on. Where cell phone opsec is concerned it can be impossible to predict who has this ability and where and when and what you can do to blend in without *looking like you're trying to blend in*. It can be a double-edged sword but, there are a few pearls I can dispense with here.

Long messages are just bad OPSEC any way you slice it. To counter this, Edward Snowden used short and punchy messages to throw off anyone trying to trace his NSA leaks back to him. This was good since if one used Tor and nothing else without care of what was previously published, it'd be pretty easy for the NSA to link him to previous documents he'd written on the open net.

As for us, we have the option of using Anonymouth. It's a tool for anonymizing every word we spit out on the open web. It's not simple to use but like PGP it can be a life saver if you need protection for any sensitive data. How does it work?

It uses Java to analyze previous works with present-day works, compares them and then tips you off to overused words, then suggests fixes to help you 'blend in'. You can even tell it to scan a folder or group of docs you'd like to 'anonymize'.

For instance. Let's say you are an Iranian political dissident using Tor. You also happen to be a journalist. Although your anonymous by way of IP address, the government in Tehran could (in theory) still analyze your anonymous posts and compare them to your known writings, say on your public blog. Same with leaking emails from a corrupt business. Maybe they'll compare what you mailed to a newspaper to all emails on a corporate server.

There's plenty of scenarios where this could be useful. It can be downloaded from the Github website at:

github.com/psal/anonymouth

FIREFOX ADDONS

These addons are presented here if none of the aforementioned apps satisfy.

Ghostery

Ghostery is very popular at the moment. What does it do? It reports all tracking packages detected (and whether Ghostery has blocked them or not) in a "findings window" accessible from clicking on the Ghostery Icon in the browser. When configured, Ghostery also displays the list of trackers present on the page in a temporary purple overlay box.

With the "Ghost rank" reporting feature enabled, Ghostery transmits the full HTML code of the page visited to Ghostery, Inc., and takes note key data such as the advertising distribution systems that users encounter and the speed at which these load on the page.

I recommend this app if you need to hide from Google. As for the NSA or Iranian government? Not a chance. According to a few online sources they sell your data. To whom or what is anyone's guess. And there are claims of this app being spyware.

But, you can prevent Ghostery from doing this by opting out of the Ghost Rank feature. The feature is opt-in so if you didn't already opt in there is nothing you need to do. If this feature bothers you, there's a few others I can recommend. One of which is PrivacyBadger. More on that one in a bit.

FlashControl

FlashControl gives you control over which sites are allowed to display the Flash player or the HTML5 player. With FlashControl installed, web content that requires Flash plugins will be disabled by default. You then enable content by clicking on a blocked area on any given webpage, or via Flashcontrol's address bar icon. You can also reblock content that you've unblocked.

This can help reduce CPU load and provide some security control so that content isn't automatically loaded without your permission.

Sidenote: I tend to walk among the block-all-flash and then click-to-play guys, but I just wish some of the video-streaming providers that use Flash would dump it and use HTML5. Then I could lead a very Flash-free life.

PRIVOXY

Privoxy is a *non-caching* web proxy with filtering capabilities for enhancing privacy, manipulating cookies and modifying web page data and HTTP headers before the page is rendered by the browser.

It's a privacy *enhancing* proxy. That is, it filters Web pages and removes advertisements. Privoxy can be customized by users for both stand-alone systems and multi-user networks and can be chained to other proxies.

It's frequently used in combination with Squid and can be used to bypass Internet censorship. Get it at the Privoxy homepage at privoxy.org.

TACO

Taco stands for Targeted Advertising Cookie Opt-Out.

This app auto-blocks hundreds of web beacons, bugs, and other tracking technologies that advertisers and others use to track you. Sounds like Ghostery to me. What it amounts to setting permanent opt-out cookies for Google and 25 others, even if those cookies are deleted by Firefox.

Now a word from our sponsor. You need to understand something about so-called "opt-out" cookies and their respective apps, which I think can be a little misleading. A couple of thoughts.

First, if you read the fine print of virtually every company's privacy policy regarding cookie use, you'll find that they promise not to display targeted ads to you based on your personal web history. That is, you'll see ads that a person would see if they were not being tracked. However, many still track you. When you start digging around in their lawyer-speak agreements you'll often find that they rarely promise that they won't track you 100%, just that they won't show you personalized ads based on their data. They still use these opt-out cookies to do any of the following:

- Track your movements, as in what sites you visit.
- What you click on.
- What you buy with credit cards or even Paypal.

Secondly, they then use this data for their own marketing purposes and may decide to sell it to other companies. So in terms of privacy, this addon by itself is inadequate without the aid of a lot of the other addons we mention - primarily because it gives people the false idea that somehow their privacy is being protected by opt-out cookies when it's not.

ADBLOCK PLUS

Adblock Plus for Firefox is the most downloaded browser extension worldwide and winner of the About.com Reader's Choice Award for 2011 and 2013, as well as the Linux New Media award for the Best Open Source Firefox Extension. Whenever I've had to re-install an OS, this is the first addon I install after Firefox.

Depending on the filter lists you have activated, you can even block YouTube video ads and Facebook tracking. Filter lists are created by members of the open source community and free to use. If you don't want to rely on filter lists you can create your own blocking rules to customize your web experience. It all sounds like a lucid dream for the budding privacy advocate.

However...

AdBlock introduced the Acceptable Ads Program a few years back. That means various companies can pay AdBlock so that their ads are added to a long 'whitelist', so that you see them in your browser. They've actually been doing this for a good while now though not many users know about it.

NOSCRIPT

NoScript allows JavaScript, Java and other executable content to run only from trusted domains of your choice. Things like your home-banking web site, guarding your "trust boundaries" against cross-site scripting attacks (XSS), cross-zone DNS rebinding / CSRF attacks (router hacking), and Clickjacking attempts, thanks to its ClearClick technology.

That's not a simple description, obviously, and for good reason since NoScript isn't a simple addon. It's very complex, but like chess is easy to learn, hard to master.

My biggest reason for using it is that NoScript users are less vulnerable to exploits than non-users. And it does a lot more than just whitelist what sites can run scripts. It also offers protection against clickjacking and cross-site scripting even if you whitelist sites. A few users even run it while globally-allowing scripts by default simply to get a few other benefits. So it's more than just a privacy tool. It's an *anonymity* tool. It comes bundled with the Tor Browser for good reason.

Another aspect I like is that the permissions function is

very domain-specific. You can allow google.com to run scripts, for instance, but deny google-analytics.com or gstatic.com. Or you can allow maps.google.com but deny all other .google.com sites. And you can even (temporarily) allow sites you'd normally deny if you need them for a specific task.

So what's the worst that could happen if you retain No Script while allowing scripts globally?

You're more vulnerable to exploits that aren't being guarded against, for one. Even if you visit a website you don't trust, scripts will still run. There'll just be some protection against dodgy techniques that you wouldn't otherwise have. And some scripts have an easier time "phoning home" and fingerprinting you. Then there's the badly-coded sites that eat up your RAM and CPU cycles.

Though there's a slight learning curve to NoScript, it isn't hard to figure out. You can block most web bugs from Facebook, Google and Twitter and the like. The 'like' button on Facebook is one such web bug. Every time you visit a site that has that button (you need not press it), a lot of data goes back to Facebook about your online habits. Same with Twitter's 'Tweet' buttons and Google's G+ buttons.

In the beginning, my biggest nitpicks were:

- Dealing with sites that want to run a gazillion scripts from a huge number of different domains, and
- How hard it was to judge the trustworthiness of third-party domains.

Obviously you must judge each site yourself according to your own opsec needs, but I solved the above two issues this way for general open net browsing:

Whenever you hit a new website, enable enough of them to get basic site functionality. Usually this means you'll allow the ones with the site name in them and work outward from there to some of the legitimate-sounding ones. Enabling past this point defeats NoScript's purpose, but you'll eventually get a feel for what you need to enable to get the site working.

UMATRIX

uMatrix is a point-and-click matrix-based firewall. Just point & click to forbid or allow any class of requests made by your browser. Not only does it block javascript, but also cookies, css, plugins, images and more on either a per domain or global basis. The interface is pretty easy, too. It exists as a plugin for both Firefox and Chrome.

Personally I like to keep NoScript for the XSS protection. uMatrix will still block javascript very well but once you allow some javascript, it will step aside. NoScript will still scan allowed javascript for obvious XSS attempts and prevent it.

uBlock Origin

uBlock Origin is a content filter by the developer of uMatrix. It shares a bit of the same functionality of uMatrix but is better suited to blocking ads. It can use the same filter lists as Adblock Plus. There's two versions: the original by Raymond Hill which has been renamed from uBlock to uBlock Origin, and a fork by Chris Aljoudi which retains the original name, uBlock.

You can use all of the above since NoScript and uMatrix often strive for the same goal. They're just fundamentally different. NoScript only blocks scripts but uMatrix blocks whole connections.

From a *privacy* perspective, uMatrix is the way to go because the connection never gets established.

From a *security* perspective, NoScript is superior. You must decide if you want to run each script. With uMatrix you can only decide on a per connection basis and NoScript won't stop third parties from connecting. Either one presents their own unique hassles. But even so, I recommend installing Privacy Badger and uBlock.

For more tools on anonymity (and a lot of other useful information) see the following link at the addon switchboard:

https://github.com/gorhill/httpswitchboard/wiki

CELL KEYLOGGERS

Keyloggers are a mixed breed of dog, and like any mixed breed I have some mixed feelings about them. They can save your hide by defending you to the death, or they can get someone's reputation or way of life destroyed.

So what's a keylogger?

It's an app that secretly records keystrokes and sends them by way of sleuthy internet magic to some evildoer on the other side of the world. Or your dad could use it to catch your mom spying on him.

They really have a million uses and, right or wrong, it is parents that are the only ones truly equipped to play Big Brother, and do so *ethically*. Certainly they've got the know-how to reign in a reckless teen who's too street-smart for his own good. Dad know the limits because Dad knows the kid inside and out. Not government. Not the FBI. And most certainly not the police.

We've seen what happens to sexting teenagers who pass around nude photos like baseball cards. It ain't pretty.

Courts and cops trawl em, raid em and jail em and then claim to 'help' the kids by throwing them on the sex offender's list because, well, that's what they like to do to *other people's kids*. I don't know about you but I think the parents can do a much better job than any bureaucrat. So below are a few I recommend if you've got a 14 year old experimenting with car jackings or gang related activity. You know, serious crimes.

For other things like weed, curfew breaking and voyeurism, I'd not recommend any of these, especially for older teens. Reason being is because they may find out their being spied on. Call it a sixth sense. Then they'll Google all kinds of ridiculous things just to toy with you. Search terms like:

- Sex change operations.
- How to make a PB&J with the crusts cut off.
- How long would a rubber duck float in the Gulf of Oman.
- My cat wants me to get an abortion.
- Is narcissism genetic?
- How do cows scratch their knees if they itch?

Stuff like that. And if you've got a kid whose intelligence rivals that of Neo in The Matrix, then you've met your match. He could get a USB stick, put a live install of Linux on it and boot from the USB drive. Keep the USB drive hidden when he isn't using it.

It's a reverse whammy unless you somehow take his stick, guess his password, figure out Ubuntu *and* find a way to install a Linux keylogger. Even if that happened, he can just format it and put a fresh copy of Ubuntu on it again.

Anyway for the uninitiated, here's the first one. It's called Spy Bubble. It monitors cell phone use on any mobile device you can think of.

After you install it, monitoring begins instantly. It'll monitor and record information on the target phone in complete stealth, giving you complete access to any sensitive information you could be looking for. At $50 bucks, it ain't free. But it's a helluva lot cheaper than hiring a lawyer.

The downside is that SpyBubble can't track stored videos or calendar events. It can't block phone numbers, websites or mobile apps. It can't set keyword alerts to send notice if the phone is used to access inappropriate material. You also can't use it to see BlackBerry Messenger chats either.

Second up is Spyera. Third is MobileSpy. Fourth is Flexispy. Fifth and last is MobiStealth.

All of these keyloggers basically do the same thing: spy on your kids, or the competing used car lot owner across the street.

DETECTING KEYLOGGERS

Detecting keyloggers isn't exactly brain surgery. You just need to know where to look. Sometimes it's difficult, but there's usually others online who've gone through the trouble of posting a thread on a forum somewhere. So help abounds. Here's a few ways you can check for keylogger modules that may have wormed their way (with a little help from the Mrs.) into your system.

Most keyloggers use a kind of DLL-injection to get under the hood and stay there without you seeing it. That means that a DLL will show up mapped to a process's address space, as seen below:

The pyd (python extension) file sits at the top in the second section under 'Name'. This one's been loaded right into Windows Explorer's address space, which means it'll run every time Explorer is run. For anything you need Explorer to do. That makes it hard to get rid of without dedicated anti-virus software that knows what to look for.

DLLs like this want to see *everything* you type, so they typically load themselves into every target address space available. For a smart cookie who knows his PC like the back of his hand, he'll likely see odd DLLs here and there that look suspicious - files he can't link to any products he's bought or uses. He can bring these up in a list for every process. Geeks do this enough every day to where they begin to see anomalies, or 'ghost files' that shouldn't be there. They don't like to rely on anti-virus programs alone.

That's one thing that kids are lousy at: noticing things like a tiny switch (or GPS device) hooked under the car ignition. Spyware companies depend on kids being uninformed.

Solutions?

1.) You can study the 'drivers' folder for any strange files.

2.) Create a debug boot file with BcdEdit and hook up a firewire cable and hit a break point when the module loads and study ALL modules, every one, filtering details as you go along. Any DLL/driver can't do squat about you looking at it before it's loaded into Windows. This is, of course, the complicated way of doing things.

3.) Almost all keyloggers phone home somewhere else. So connect to a transparent proxy and note connections not familiar to you. You may see something along the lines of 'myspy.ukraine.com' rather than just your usual VPN address.

4.) Purchase an 'anti-keylogger' program. There as numerous as anti-virus vendors, but not all equal.

Obviously if you're using this spyware to monitor your kids, they won't have half the brainpower to do any of the above unless they've got a few whiz kids in their circle of friends. Better safe than sorry, I'm with the parents on this one.

TOR AND CELL PHONES

Tor users generally fall into one of two categories: The average Joe who can't be bothered to expand his knowledge of security past an intermediate level is one of them. He's super confident, and generally he likes things easy-peasy. Press a button and go. Many Mac users used to fall into this category but now many Windows users get overconfident in their own security abilities.

The other group are Tor superhackers who can smell a Tor honeypot from Hong Kong to Longview, Texas. They know when the cops are around. Hounds, they are. They can smell the red-blue, red-blue of a police cruiser's lights long before they come on.

While their numbers are few, they're also the restless types since they can't sleep unless they've plugged every security hole imaginable and chained enough proxies to circle the moon. Even then they're generally the most paranoid obsessed micro-managers this side of a psych ward. We aim to be somewhere in the middle.

But you should know that even with the anonymous Tor browser, anonymity on a cell phone is harder than on a PC because of how phones are now entwined with social media applications and your real identity. This, along with how Google loves to track every move you make (even if you whistle a copyrighted tune out your backside), makes smartphone opsec very problematic indeed for the survivalist and anonymity enthusiast.

But first, a refresher on the basics.

Tor & IP Addresses

I'll repeat this a million times if necessary: Your IP address is worth GOLD to social media giants like Facebook and YouTube.

Think about the long-term effects of monitoring you for years on end for a moment.

Your browser alone, never mind all the leaks of data your OS gives, provides all kinds of data on your lifestyle by way of web analytics. Things like where you like to shop, what you say and to whom you say it and how often. Which political or religious forums you frequent. Your pets names. Your hairdresser. Your fixer.

And that's not all. It links your family history on social media sites. It links your favorite book genres, your favorite sexual fantasies, your eye color. The list goes on and on. Therefore it is most crucial that we hide it as much as possible as we build out our cellular fortress of doom from which nothing can penetrate. If you don't know what Tor is, I highly recommend visiting the Tor website to learn the dirty little details.

The gist of this is that any packet sent by Tor is stripped of the sender's originating info. Tor is able to remove who sent the packet and who the intended recipient is. Think of it this way:

Imagine you sent an envelope to person A, and in that envelope was an envelope to send to person B.

- Person A then sends the letter to person B.

- B gets the envelope from A, and in that envelope is *another* envelope to send to person C.

- Person C gets that envelope from B, then looks up the information that is requested. Then that person sends the response in an envelope addressed to person B.

- Person B puts that in an envelope for A and sends to A, which then puts it in another envelope to send back to you.

Tor routing works like this, except you also know the public keys for A, B, and C ahead of time, so that when you send a message to person A, the only thing that A can decrypt is the fact you are sending a message to B - only the message itself is **still encrypted** and **only decryptable by Person C**. Meanwhile, Person B receives, decrypts, and relays the message to C but never knows you sent it, and C has no idea who you or "A" really is.

If you're in the United States, there's some bad news to hear. Tor is generally safer for citizens that don't live in nations with lots of alphabet agencies (i.e. intelligence) running Tor exit nodes that sniff traffic. If you're in the USA and run Tor - as long as no one is deploying high statistical traffic-analysis on you, your IP address is generally safe for the session. Given enough resources and time/funding, Tor can be not-very-safe if your doing anything illegal.

That said, this leaves a lot to be desired when we need good opsec. So many ways exist that could out your identity. If you open Hotmail for instance while surfing with Tor, any alphabet agency can, with sufficient resources, correlate that address with Tor activity. Keyloggers can too. They can record keystrokes outside of Tor and send them online to destinations unknown. From Russia with Love. You could even run into a site that has an XSS security hole and have your identity stolen right out from under you. A million things could go wrong.

For this reason, we need to set a few ground rules for using Tor. It doesn't matter what you're using it for. Americans have been arrested for sarcastic comments left on Facebook. So anything done on Tor must never be connected with any social media outlet. Ever.

10 TOR RULES FOR SMARTPHONE USERS

The way we go about securing our phone with Tor is to assume everything you run is compromised. Plug all the holes so to speak. And the basic guidelines are the same.

- **No Browser Customizations** - That is, no customization based on emotional whims. The Tor Browser can't fix your personal imprint that drip-feeds intel onto the net, which leads to your front door in the same way a wolf leaves dribbles of urine back to it's lair. Plugins like Flash, QuickTime and Firefox Personas can reveal your IP address. Load up Firefox with a dozen social media plugins and you can kiss your anonymity goodbye. This also means no YouTube. No Facebook. No Twitter. No LinkedIn.
- **Avoid Chrome and Internet Explorer** - There's no reason to use these at all since Tor comes pre-bundled with a very fine-tuned Firefox setup. Chrome isn't built for Tor. It's built for tracking you. That's what Google does. Google didn't

build a billion dollar search empire by playing nice. Just as Samsung when they tried to sneak an Adblock-like app into the Play Store. They did reinstate it later but not without some heavy oversight.

- **Never Open Executables** - If I absolutely must run an executable file, pdf or document, I transfer it to memory stick and carry it by hand to a computer that is not online. I then copy/paste it to a virtual machine like VMWare with Windows installed (aka sandboxed) so that if a virus does exist, it's ability to do damage is limited. Think of a nuclear weapon going off underground out in the Nevada desert.
- **Use Tor Bridges** - If Tor brings to much heat, use a Bridge Relay. While vanilla Tor does a good job, it's not perfect. It can't prevent an NSA data center with huge resources from doing traffic analysis to determine if your using Tor. If you want to hide the fact you're using Tor, then opt for a Tor Bridge Relay instead of a direct connection to the same Tor entry point everyone else uses.
- **Act Like Everybody Else** - Tor relayed this to me that when I maximized Tor Browser:

Maximizing Tor Browser can allow websites to determine your monitor size, which can be used to track you.

The solution is simple. Always use the default options whenever possible unless it enhances anonymity, such as disabling Javascript. One comment on the Tor Blog illuminates why this is the case:

"Using an unusual screen resolution was sufficient to

identify me uniquely to Panopticlick.com. With my portrait mode screen resolution of 1200 wide by 1920 high, the default window size of 1000x1765 was unique, no resizing or maximizing needed."

A website can find out information about your screen that includes width, height, DPI, color depth, and even font smoothing. A 1080p resolution isn't so bad, but the worst thing you can do is to resize the Tor browser to a random size instead of maximizing it. Any adversary won't have a clue about the hardware you're running, but you'll probably be the only person with that browser size on each site you visit.

This is bad since it means your activity can be tracked - the adversary will know that sites A, B and C were visited by the same person despite the fact that Tor used three different IPs to access those sites.

Therefore, act like everybody else.

- **Never enter your real information online.** Perhaps this is obvious, but don't enter in anything that may reveal your identity online. If asked for your personal details when signing up for a web site, lie.
- **Take extra caution if you register a domain name.** If you want to set up a site of your own, you may be tempted to register your own domain. Be careful. Domain name registrars collect a lot of information and reveal a lot in WHOIS records. If you register a domain name, do so anonymously.

ANONYMOUS ANDROID: MISSION IMPOSSIBLE

Strong anonymity takes a lot of hard work as you'll soon find out. It's like something out of Pandora's Box.

Securing a leaky, soul-stealing privacy-eating gremlin-toothed operating system like Android can unleash hell quite easily. And all it takes is one mistake, a simple curiosity, a little peek that leads to another, and another and before you know it you're one cocky, self-absorbed son of a gun who can do no wrong when the inevitable happens. You take unnecessary risks.

What happens to those on a motorcycle who take risks? Gun owners? Athletes?

The day you lose respect is the day you'll wind up beneath an overturned gasoline tanker. Like chess and motorcycles, it's just not an easy platform to master. In fact, Android is a pain in the ass to lock down, a beast that doesn't like chains and being told what to do. Just when you think you've got her figured out, she shapeshifts.

Changing Android's Hardware (firmware)

Your phone or tablet has two operating systems. One on top, such as iOS or Android, and one beneath that deals with all things radio. That's the beast in the basement we must deal with if we are to sail the flagship named Anonymity.

It's housed in firmware and gets its meat from a baseband processor, so it's a little difficult to access without modifications. Make that, *dangerous* modifications.

Most of them run on the ARM processor but that's of little consequence since you can replace the Android operating system itself if you so desire. You can do this by installing CyanogenMod along with Team Win Recovery Project.

Required apps:
- CyanogenMod
- Team Win Recovery Project image
- F-Droid package
- Orbot from F-Droid
- Droidwall from F-Droid
- Droidwall Firewall Scripts

HOW TO ACCESS HIDDEN ONION SITES ON THE DEEP WEB

Onion sites are those sites with an .onion extension that can only be reached by using the Tor Browser. You cannot reach them on the open web. Accessing them is just like accessing any other site over the Tor network as long as you know the address.

To that end, Reddit holds a repository of interesting darknet articles and a massive number of darknet links in the sidebar.

LINUX DARKNET EDITION

Linux Darknet is just a fancy term for Tails, The Amnesic Incognito Live System. It uses the Linux operating system and comes highly recommended. Bruce Schneier and Ed Snowden along with a host of other well-known security experts cannot praise it's strengths enough. It's cheap, fast, and untraceable even for those new to the Deep Web. As a matter of fact, it's the perfect incognito tool for doing *anything* on the Deep Web.

What You Need:

- A PC or laptop capable of running a live operating system via USB/DVD.
- A Blank DVD or USB Stick
- A 4GB Stick for Persistence (In case you want to create a persistent volume in the free space left on the device by Tails Installer. The files in the persistent volume are saved encrypted and remain available across separate working sessions).

One of the great things about Tails is that it forgets *everything* at shutdown. All files, settings, and RAM are cleared. When you need permanent storage, a USB or SD card can be used. More than likely you *will* have sensitive info on this storage, so it should also be encrypted.

How to Setup Tails

Warning: Never run Tails in a Virtual Machine. Doing so jeopardizes your security as you put yourself at the mercy of the host operating system. Whonix is a much better option for this, which I go into detail in my Tor & the Dark Art of Anonymity book. One reason is spelled out on the Tails website:

"Both the host operating system and the virtualization software are able to monitor what you are doing in Tails."

Which means "If the host operating system is compromised with a software keylogger or other malware, then it can break the security features of Tails".

Another reason is that traces of your Tails session are likely to be left on the local hard disk. For example, host operating systems usually use swapping (or paging) which copies part of the RAM to the hard disk.

- Download the Tails ISO image from the Tails website.
- Verify the image

Now choose which to boot from. You've 2 choices: USB or DVD.

You now need to edit the Boot Order. Depending on your computer you should see an entry for removable drive or USB media. Move this to the top of the list to force the computer to attempt to start from your device before starting from the hard disk. Disable Fast boot and Secure boot, then click save and continue.

You should see the Tails operating system after rebooting. Now feel free to hack the Pentagon to see if Area 51 really was the site of a crashed UFO.

On system shutdown, make sure everything you need is saved either to an external encrypted drive or your Persistence. Upper right corner has the power off button. Click and select shutdown to turn off.

- Alternatively: Remove USB to initiate shutdown.

- Wait for the RAM to be wiped.

- Done. You have completed a secure session with Tails. Everything not saved has been lost and is irretrievable.

Tails is the most respected privacy app out there for good reason. It leaks the least data of every system in existence and is scrutinized *mercilessly*. Whonix is also a good choice, but it is less used and thus less scrutinized. Therefore you should use Tails as a starting point on your journey that is the Darknet Marketplace - which we'll descend into next.

BYPASSING WEBSITES THAT BLOCK TOR

I'll keep this short and sweet. By now you know that Tor isn't foolproof, especially on cell phones.

It's just a lock on your shed after all, a lock designed to make you a harder target than the next guy. Websites know this, even adversarial ones who do not like Tor users.

Plenty of websites will block any IP address associated with Tor, even if it is not an exit node. The sites you want to use may already be listed in there.

But exit nodes are not hidden. In order to hide your Tor usage you need to proxy-chain a VPN so that any traffic coming out isn't coming from a known Tor node.

You can see a list of exit nodes here:

https://check.torproject.org/cgi-bin/TorBulkExitList.py?ip="YOURIP"

In most cases they may only be able to block the largest and most used exit nodes, but if you cannot access a particular website, use their own tools against them by configuring Tor (via the torrc file) to use an exit node that recently joined the network (up to a few hours or days, whichever you need).

You'll sneak into the castle and past the anti-Tor drawbridge because it takes time for a website to update the Tor block list.

If on the other hand you'd like to setup Tor to only use exit nodes from a specific country (like the USA for example), then you need to look for the torrc file inside the Tor Browser directory (Data/Tor/) and add this line to the torrc file using a text editor:

ExitNodes {us}

CAN THE GOVERNMENT TRACK WHICH SITES I VISIT OVER TOR?

Tor's design document Section 3.1 states:

A global passive adversary is the most commonly assumed threat when analyzing theoretical anonymity designs. But like all practical low-latency systems, Tor does not protect against such a strong adversary.

If you've got three-letter agencies after you and they have a special interest in obtaining your data, it'd be easier to just deliver a payload remotely by way of a keylogger and, failing that, done covertly with assistance from local LE where they may send out an unmarked car to initiate surveillance of your property.

These days, especially in the United States, any judge will gladly take the two seconds it requires to sign a subpoena if law enforcement waves a few colorful alarm words at them (terrorism, child porn, survivalist gremlins), with many judges not bothering to ask whether or not you're simply using Tor to help the network out.

For most users, Tor provides the best available protection against a well-resourced
observer. It's an open question how much protection Tor (or any other existing anonymous communications tool) provides against the NSA's large-scale Internet surveillance. On its own, Tor can't protect against attacks against vulnerabilities on your computer or its software.

If the adversary is the NSA, a seriously strong SIGINT entity, the best offense is a good defense – being a pain in the neck to target. That's the goal. You must look and act like everyone else because it disrupts the intelligence-gathering cycle. A well-funded SIGINT entity like the NSA won't waste time going over your cleartext communications since your metadata & ID patterns are good enough. That's why any agency worth its salt will be much better at *targeting* than crypto-analysis.

For this reason you should always use Tor on something other than a cell phone if you can help it. Reason being is that they monitor everything they can get their paws on before feeding this data into the beast system for whatever endgame their planning. There's no doubt anymore on this.

And until the night of the long knives and we see enemies of the state strung up by their feet (like those old black and white photos), there will be no end to data harvesting.

Onionscan may be of some use to check for security holes.

TOR & SMS VERIFICATION

Like the annoying buzz of a fly, Tor users have to deal with SMS verifications to register for a website on occasion. Hidden services as well, it seems, must deal with it, even merchants.

Be very careful with this. Optimally your threat model should not require any such 'verification' outside the usual opsec tools. Exposing yourself (by way of a cell) in this way not only grants the media sites you visit a nice gourmet of your metadata, but any network operator, law enforcement or hacker may join in for a bite if you use the same cell to login to social media sites. Until we have traceless SMS, I'd avoid that site for anything requiring anonymity.

But for Darknet Marketplaces, take a gander below. It's a hypothetical scenario involving a Tor user who wants to buy from a Black Market vendor. Who cares what he wants to buy. That's his business. But the vendor in question has a decent reputation on Agora Marketplace, so the customer sends over his PGP info (encrypted of course).

Vendor: That PGP data didn't make it through. Use SMS4Tor ok? (he sends the link).

Customer: I'll just resend PGP using the profile key you gave.

Vendor: Still ain't workin, pal. Dunno why not cuz you ordered last week.

Customer: Last week? Wasn't me as I've never ordered from you. Will you resend that public key again so I can import it (again) and re-send?

Vendor: Methinks you're using a different PGP app. Same as last week. (he then issues more demands)

Notice anything off about the above conversation? I do. The vendor is an incompetent clown. Two PGP apps not compatible? That's something either a cop or hacker might say to get more information (i.e. fishing). It's the same tactic Homeland Security uses when they infiltrate chat rooms and try to fish for some new meat who's a first-time buyer.

Whether incompetence comes by way of a hacker or an incompetent stooge vendor, never jeopardize your safety by assuming they are just having an 'off day' and blow it off. Follow your gut, always.

TOR PRANKS & CELL PHONES

There are a lot of bored college students out there who believe Tor makes for one seriously strong suit of armor against any and all would-be opponents, and an invisible one at that. An invisible knight is, well, pretty formidable foe. Maybe these jesters just feel they were born in the wrong century. Regardless, we can learn a lot from their folly. You, o' anonymous traveler, must use the gift of discernment to rightly divide fantasy from reality because what works in the world of Faerun doesn't squire well with the real world. Case in point:

A Harvard kid decided he wasn't quite prepared for final exams, so he emailed a bomb threat to get out of taking them. He used Tor and a throwaway email account to cover his online footprint, only little did he know that all the school officials had to do was search through the campus lab's logs to discern who accessed Tor at that time. It led them straight to his dorm room.

It probably didn't help that he used Harvard's WiFi to access Tor. He was the only one who did at that particular time.

If you are at a Mardi Gras party and everyone else has removed their masks except you, you're going to stand out. If you want to be anonymous, then use tools that enable you to look like everyone else *when everyone else is using it*. Our Harvard friend did not. Imagine yourself paying cash for something small. Cash is considered king for anonymity but can backfire if you're the only one using it to pay for a brand new Camaro in a 200 mile radius.

Recall what Kevin Mitnick (hacker wanted by the FBI) said upon his arrest; that Tsutomu Shimomura, a computer security expert, had broken the 'rules' by helping the Feds nab him instead of relying on his technical expertise – and nothing else. He thought it a game and any attack vector would come through Tor and Tor alone. For this reason you mustn't think of anonymity as some fantasy game with a ruleset. Cops do not play by the rules. They play dirty. They break the rules. They break the law. Then they break you because you think they are confined by their own laws. Only they are not.

Any action, especially a cell phone prank like that of our Harvard genius, leaves breadcrumbs for others to follow. When you use WiFi at Starbucks for example, then you are there in the flesh doing the deed and in well range of CCTV surveillance. There are fingerprints on your coffee cup; the same you pitched into the trashcan alongside your slightly used comb.

So blend in to the detriment of comfort. Avoid layers of anonymity that produce complex requirements yet produce more visibility. Ninjas in ancient Japan did not look like the sort of ninja Chuck Norris went toe to toe against in The Octagon.

They didn't wear black pajamas. They looked like your neighborly rice farmer, one among dozens of other rice farmers.

BLACK MARKETS ON THE DEEP WEB

Here are a few things you can buy on the Deep Web you may not have heard about.

- Rare Opsec Manuals for Survivalists
- Rare Special Ops Guides
- 3D Printed Guns and Bullets
- Drugs for Cancer
- Japanese Manga
- Books on How to Overthrow Governments

Top Darknet Markets

THERE ARE two types of Blackmarket Drug emporiums on the Deep Web. Those you trust and those you don't. Below is a list of some of the more popular black market outlets. One or two may be gone already by the time this book goes to press. In five years all of them may be gone. The point here isn't to steer you into any one of these in particular or even that I want you to buy illegal drugs (I don't), but to remind you that none of these sites will last forever just as Google and Microsoft won't last forever.

SOMETHING WILL COME ALONG to replace the behemoths just as surely the same as AltaVista, Infoseek, Napster and Divx were replaced. It can happen quick. My grandfather's motto: Never gamble or invest more than you can afford to lose.

Agora Marketplace

Established: Dec 3, 2013
Invite (Required)

Abraxas Market

Established: Dec 13, 2014
Invite (Required)

Nucleus Market

Established: Nov 24, 2014

Middle Earth Marketplace

Established: Jun 22, 2014

The Russian Anonymous Marketplace (aka RAMP)

Established: Unknown

MARKETPLACE INVITES

You may have noticed that a handful of these markets, such as Agora, require <u>invites</u>. What this means is if you're a new buyer or vendor or even just a nosy parker lurking around, you cannot register without an invite link from an already registered user. That's just how it is with some of the more established outlets.

Also, don't assume that because a website's been around longer than the others that it is more secure, and never assume that a closed door means it is closed forever, or for even a long time. At Agora for instance, you'll sometimes see this error:

"Cannot register at this time, user limit reached. Please wait until full time release."

It's confusing because it's meant to be. They try to be as cryptic as possible to throw off anyone looking to take them down. The first option is to either sit tight for a few hours and give the server time to catch it's breath, or...

- Visit the forum of the marketplace you're trying to reach and ask for an invite. Failing this, you can

- Visit the Reddit subforum of the market in question.

Two points to say on this.

First, if you're using a long term account and login using Tor, then your activity can build a profile of sorts, all based on what you do on the Reddit site. Tor can't really prevent this from happening so if you want to *preserve your anonymity*, you must keep your 'real' identity and 'hidden' identity completely separate. One way is to never log into any account with both identities.

The second point about Reddit is merely a suggestion:

Beware of *phishing* links there, both on related as well as non-Darknet related subreddits. All referral links are safe as long as the link begins with the official Agora URL. Anything else is likely a phishing link. And the person whose referral link you use doesn't get any "notifications" or anything letting them know you used it, nor can they see how many people used their link. You are completely anonymous to them.

If you can remember two phone numbers, then you can remember 16-characters for an official link. If you still can't be bothered, there's a third option.

3.) Visit clearnet sites that spell out where the site is and even have rating systems in place.

Just be warned that they, like many hidden servers across the Deep Web, come and go like the tide. Some will even change their .onion address for security reasons and some will go down as felled trees because of DDOS attacks, hacking attempts or that gut feeling you get when the spider you threw behind the dresser in the wee morning hours is now looking at you from across the room like he wants to skate down your spine with a flamethrower.

In other words, always assume someone is watching.

THE BLACKMARKET SUPERLIST

If you're curious about what other sites exist further down the rabbit hole, you can find the Superlist at:

https://i.reddit.com/r/DarkNetMarkets/wiki/superlist

It's a list of "all currently known, operating markets and tumblers" with the disclaimer that "all markets listed should not be taken as endorsements or confirmation by the moderators that a market is trusted. Always confirm links before you use them."

Requirements for this superlist are as follows:

- The Market must have been up for at least a week after announcing themselves on Reddit's DarknetMarket page.
- The Market has to have at least 20 listings from active vendors.
- Their service must have at least 50% uptime over the span of a week, under moderator discretion.

- Users must be able to withdraw their bitcoins (or other relative currency).

SHIPPING & RECEIVING: THOU SHALT NOTS

What follows are a few pearls of wisdom from which you may benefit, chief among them being the use of your real-life details; things like your name, address, phone number, Facebook profile, what have you, that many newbies pass around like skittles. Too much transparency can be catastrophic to any Darknet Marketplace or even a single purchase, especially when dealing with a place like Agora.

- If the doorbell rings and you give the delivery guy a fake name, a warning bell is going to go off in his head that you're the next Silk Road admin looking to fill his coffers. He knows your real name already, so don't lie unless you want him to file a report. If your wife has sticky fingers from opening your mail, buy a private box at the UPS store or post office.
- It's okay to use a fake name if you've got the credentials to back it up. Fake passports can be bought online as gag gifts that wouldn't fool a TSA officer but *would* fool the mailman and

maybe even the UPS store employee. I rented one in Canada and the female employee looked to be no older than 23 years old. She wasn't very observant with details. They won't call the cops on you either way.

- Agora cannot send drones to deliver your package. Therefore you need to realize that sensitive materials requiring anonymous services take longer. If you order in December, expect a delay but don't pester the help desk people unless it's been two weeks since you ordered. For every commonsense person out there who can follow instructions, there's a million pigeons who have the solution right under their beaks. The solution is a little dove called Patience.

- Use PGP for any and all messages. This is because your address is connected with a Darknet Marketplace and by extension, a vendor who sells items of dubious legality. A hundred things can go wrong. One being the site can be imaged by police with your fancy cul-de-sac address being front and center along with every sentence you've uttered (use short sentences!). A few vendors won't even talk to you if you refuse to encrypt. So use GPG4USB to save yourself the rejection slips. It only takes 20 minutes to learn.

- Bitcoin Tumblers. Assuming you bought Bitcoins connected to your real-life identity, you should wash or 'tumble' them BEFORE you buy. That means putting those coins through a tumbler like Coinbase first before any depositing goes on at the Agora address. If you withdraw from Agora, it's the reverse procedure:

Agora account to tumbler to Coinbase and *then* into your Bitcoin Wallet.

- Which Bitcoin Tumblers, you ask? Well, the most stable ones you can find. For 2016 onward, Grams Helix Light is the top choice, al though you're hit with a 2.5% fee for the total cost. BitBlender is also a good choice but they require account setups. SharedCoin is yet another but I found it makes it harder to figure out who sent bitcoins to what address. It uses a different method of relaying than the others. This is primarily for small buyers, not for someone looking to pack a warehouse with marijuana bricks in Chicago, Illinois.
- It may come to pass that you've ordered something and haven't received it yet. It's been ages. Have you been scammed? Locked out of your account? Or maybe your bitcoins never showed up in your Agora account? Don't fall on your sword just yet. What you need to do is message the market admins, not any forum at Ars Technica or Reddit or anyplace else, and send a (private) message to 'Agora' detailing your problem. The backlog of tickets is considerable but they will get back to you in 48 hours, usually. They tend to bump you further down the priority list if you go overboard and start issuing threats, however, so don't burn any bridges by giving them any catitude.

TO FINALIZE EARLY OR NOT?

I explored this topic in my Tor and the Dark Art of Anonymity book and I'll mention it here, albeit briefly.

Opsec lessons can be costly. Finalize Early, which means you pay a vendor *before* you receive the magical goods, can wreck your life like none other. In general you should avoid ever doing this since the risks alone will give you an ulcer.

Many before you can attest to getting ripped off to the tune of five figures or more. Vendors can build up trust a long time before they bolt with the bitcoins, a scheme called Exit Scamming. That's when the vendor, a sneering twirly-mustached little man works his black magic and makes off with the loot. *Your* loot.

Newcomers like to trust them implicitly not to rip them off, until they do. Then they spam Usenet, Reddit, Ars Technica and every other tech site with doom and gloom as though said evil man set off a tactical nuke in New Jersey.

Most online places all have trackable systems in place that, when linked with those utilized by credit card companies and banks, can save your hide and get you your stolen funds back. Sometimes. Darknet Marketplaces don't however. If you get robbed then it's highly likely you won't be getting your money back *and* you'll likely not be alone in that regard.

400 positive feedbacks sounds like a lot of happy customers. Only it isn't. A vendor with thousands of deals under his belt would be a lot of happy customers IF he has a good rating to boot and IF you've done your research, but even then it doesn't justify losing every coin you own.

INTERNATIONAL VS. DOMESTIC ORDERS

Pride goeth before destruction, and an haughty spirit before a fall
- Proverbs 16:18

I always like to remember that verse when I travel overseas. It's to remind myself not to get too cocky in foreign markets.

Do you travel overseas? Have a passport? Bank cards? Email? Imagine that every day you wake up every little thing that happens to you has to be looked at with suspicion. Emails from family. Your new girlfriend. Whenever the phone rings. That's what it is to be a slave, a slave to your own ego.

You may think there's something magical about buying illegal items from international ports of call. Don't believe the hype. It's the same tune but with twice the headache. Whether international falls into the "Thou Shalt" or "Shalt Not" category is up to you of course, but how many migraines do you want? One lump or twenty? Can you lose it all without losing your sanity? Do you want it quick or safe and secret?

Turkey and the Netherlands brings with it more potency but increased security. Increased security means higher risk. Higher risk means more intense pain.

Content from these exotic locales draw unwanted attention and stand out from other packages unless some extensive pre-made cover has been setup. Australia comes to mind. It's riskier than other places. The biggest risk is where the Deep Web intersects with the international Real World - and getting the stuff delivered to you - and keeping you and your family safe.

A few pointers:

- NEVER check the status of a package through Tor. Packages tracked via Tor are automatically flagged.

- Never send contraband from a state where it is legal (i.e. Colorado).

- If you're a vendor, never plaster your site with the word "Cheap!!" and then try and slide in heavy shipping costs at the last second. Customers hate that.

- Don't use first.last@gmail.com as your email address, as other dumb people have (though granted Ross didn't know he was creating a Black Market Superstore, nor did he have any knowledge of the Snowden/Prism/LOLsec revelations).

- No teams. EVERYONE cooperates or you can't operate = not likely. Also, any website that must rely on distribution via US mail is going to have a very bad day. Couriers are better.

An international buy is much the same as domestic except it comes with substantially higher risk and has the added value that you can be extradited to the other country after the U.S asset forfeiture laws clean your carcass of any link to humanity - assuming there's anything left since the U.S.A is the prison capitol of the world.

BLACK MARKET ARRESTS

We've seen what happens with money and ego. One always prevails over the other. Watch the film Heat starring Al Pacino. One guy on the team of thieves, the new guy, gets everyone else killed or close to it. His bad opsec destroys everyone else's good opsec; the rotten apple or yeast parable applies here: A little bad ruins the whole dough.

There's one site I found quite informative in this department. It lists every black market arrest imaginable. Interestingly the list omits a glaring data set: one that involves each darknet market operator's OPSEC - admittedly hard to quantify. Take Silk Road for instance. From the link we can deduce that opsec just isn't that high a priority for some users.

"No single theme emerges reading through the many arrests. Some people are busted through sheer bad luck in being randomly pulled over or their packages inspected; some are undone by other peoples' mistakes, and some have no one but themselves to blame for talking to a policeman and blurting out all their secrets; some

are undone by their trust in others, and some are undone by lying to federal agents; some are undone by signing for packages, while others are undone by a stray fingerprint; some followed the OPSEC rules and some engaged in mind-boggling follies like using their real return address or accepting payment to their own bank account or running their own clearnet site; some clammed up, denied everything, and saved themselves, while others kept records of everything (perhaps in the misguided belief it would earn them clemency in the worst) and only condemned themselves; some were busted at home, others in the totalitarian zones of international borders; some were busted through high-tech browser-based deanonymization, but most through low-tech methods like a customer or friend snitching; some sellers' packages are spotted during Customs inspections, and some are noticed only when delivery fails & the bogus return addresses explode."

OPSEC FOR BUYERS

Mark Twain once stated, "I don't like to commit myself about heaven and hell. You see, I have friends in both places."

OPSEC is more important than anything else when it comes to buying Darknet product. You can never have enough, so it's a little like ammo. If you were in Ukraine when the Soviets invaded would you be better off playing the part of sniper or just cutting bait and running? Sometimes you just have to do both. Allow me to run through a few truths that make this a little more applicable.

Your Machine is Your Fortress

Tor is a fine tool for playing cloak and dagger with small purchases, but it isn't suitable for large orders or running from the FBI. Given what's happened in the U.S. and UK over the last 5 years even small orders may be detrimental to your freedom. And free speech. Government bureaucrats have all but guaranteed they respect neither the Constitution nor our laws.

So then. What can we learn from Silk Road? Well first off, there's evidence that Silk Road's servers were misconfigured and revealing IP addresses and that they were doing it repeatedly. The index page gave away the IP address for several minutes via a print_r debug message printed to every requesting browser. That's the online goofs, but you can screw up offline, too.

Silk Road Lessons

1.) Your encryption keys to your drives are as sacred as your PGP keys. Do not give them out. Not to your roommate, your girlfriend or your mother, and especially not to your friends. Not even your business partner Eddie.

2.) Leave your PC unattended at your own peril. With your OS booted and up and running, anyone from thieves to cops to jealous girlfriends can access anything on your hard drive that isn't nailed as tight as a coffin (i.e. encrypted containers).

3.) Talk at your own PERIL. That is, never mention darknet marketplaces to anyone. Feign ignorance. While you needn't do a disappearing act like Bilbo Baggins did, telling one person will almost always have the same effect as telling a dozen people, all strangers. And it almost always is valuable to someone, somewhere.

4.) Keep your Darknet Marketplace username/pass under lock and key. Write it down in a text file but encrypt it with Veracrypt or PGP. No stickies.

5.) Use different username/passwords for different markets.

Psych Tricks

The following are merely suggestions, nothing more, and are more apt to apply to creative types over say, mathematicians.

Music: Certain kinds of music reproduce specific kinds of behavior. Stephen King listens to AC/DC when he writes. He cranks it up. Personally I feel an aneurism coming on if I try to write to that. So I listen to Steve Roach, ambient composer with titles like Dreamtime Return and Early Man. Dreamy wispy music. It works. If I switch it up then I lose focus and get distracted too easily.

Light/Darkness: In almost every scene in The Matrix, Neo can be seen always working in the dark. Even his display glows a matrix-green with cryptic lettering, the only brightness in the room being that of his monochrome skin. Works for me too. Almost like a sensory-deprivation chamber and it's amazing how much better I sleep because of it.

Locale: Stephen King once said that you don't need a glamorous 'study' to write good stories. You just need something familiar. And he's right. Having traveled to a few countries I can tell you that writing in a new city every week is not remotely possible for me as there's just too many distractions. You need a spot like Neo did - a place your identity always goes but never goes *outside of* either by doorway or otherworldly portal.

Drugs: Caffeine, nicotine, sugar highs, but no prescription drugs. They put me in a state of mind that gets reinforced daily, though I do toss and turn at night. Alcohol, Stephen King once stated, helps immensely with epic fiction writing but kills you in the process. I can vouch for that.

Scents: My girlfriend used to light caramel candles to scent up the room whenever she'd come over from the ER, usually when I was just finishing up a mindblowing chapter. After the breakup I had trouble finishing chapters.

The point of all of this is this: the more opsec you employ on a daily basis, the more your brain will, IF put into action, develop an opsec-focused mindset that doesn't have to be turned on every day. It just kicks in. Automatic. Razor sharp as piranha teeth. It does this because it's burned in like ram on a motherboard. Like pushing a button to boot Linux, you open your eyes and it's there, waiting for orders. It'll be there especially when any dangerous developments present themselves. Develop and hone this and you won't mistake that woodpecker at 6 AM for a group of angry white-hot stormtroopers.

Engaging in shady deals is a little like gambling. The house always wins if you keep playing. If you can't work the opsec well then the only winning move, as Matthew Broderick found out in Wargames, is not to play. If you continue to play recklessly, it'll be tough to find a lawyer who takes payment in bitcoins.

VENDOR OPSEC

You get what you pay for, and playing cheap gets expensive if you're caught. For any Tor hidden server operator, that means never letting the reins fall into someone else's hands. Not your associates, your girlfriend or cousin Eddie because it's you and you alone they're coming after, lock stock and barrel.

One torpedo can wipe out an entire battleship and they only have to get lucky once. You can't afford a lucky strike, so you as captain need to sense when something's 'off' so you can pull the plug without having to explain why. Partners will demand to know why of course, but it's better to run silent and deep.

Ross Ulbricht failed in this department. But we can learn a lot from his mistakes.
    Looking through the court details of his arrest one gets the impression that he was not only lax in basic IT security, but that he knew nothing about how search engines track users at all. So Lady Luck never really had to come into the

FBI's playbook at all. The guy was just sloppy and might as well have slapped on the cuffs himself.

Ross was caught long before Silk Road grew mega-popular. Court documents reveal security mistakes that a rookie drug dealer on Miami Vice might have made, not someone in charge of a multi-million dollar Deep Web drug operation. Here are a few of Ross's opsec blunders.

- Advertising openly on the Bitcoin Talk forum that he needed an IT guy for a hidden Tor service - and then using his real name for a Gmail address *and* his Silk Road Wordpress site, a site he connected to from outside of Tor.

- Ross's Google Plus account connected to his Gmail with a list of his favorite Austrian economic theory videos, the same theories he'd bragged about using for Silk Road on more than one clearnet forum.

- Using code for SilkRoad from a public programming site (i.e. StackOverflow), from an account never accessed with Tor with his IP address being out in the open for months. Any law enforcement official could track these breadcrumbs at their leisure.

- Using his real identity on LinkedIn, with links to Silk Road musings on his Wordpress blogs.

These are just some of the mistakes he made, to say nothing about his lax hidden server settings. Besides these, there's a lot to be said for smart vendors who know good security.

Vendor Guidelines Part I

These are just like the buyer opsec rules, except in reverse. Short and sweet.

- Use a sanitized laptop, cash bought, with only a Linux distro configured to run Tor and *only* Tor, with no other outgoing connections allowed.

- Dissolving your real-life persona and using different usernames on every forum visited with no non-Tor IP addresses exposed.

- Not residing in the USA. This is a big one.

- No ordering of fake IDs in the USA (vendors only) or any other contraband that'd raise suspicion with authorities.

Vendor Guidelines, Part II

So then. You've read this far and want to be a vendor or at least know what it takes to be one and not get caught.

This is **very shady territory**. Mostly illegal.

There's no accidents here. No 'accidentally' slipping on rings found in dark, damp caves. No 'but I was only looking for UFOs' excuses. Success in the black arts tends to fuel a life of it's own much like Sauron's ring of Power. It's knowledge that *wants* to be abused. Before we discuss the criminal element, let's discuss the business side of things.

- You have to be a businessman. If you're smart you should consider investing $500 and take an introduction course at the university. Do it online. You'll need to know the ins and outs of mail-order, accounts and ledgers (and when to dispose of them), and how to replenish your products. Doing it all anonymously raises the difficulty by a factor of ten. It's hard work even when it's legal products.

- Sell fakes at first. Cubic zirconium rings. Flour. Fake credit cards. Not to real customers but to *yourself*, and long before any real product matures.

- Money talks. Invest in a site that charges a fee for vendors. People take you seriously when they know you've got startup capital.

- Create a Dark Persona. This is the hardest part of all, as this person must be the opposite of the real You in every detail: Politics. Sexual taste. Movies. Style. Age. Locale. Accent. If you're confused on what this means, watch The Matrix. Neo lives two lives and the Agents know it. It's why it was so hard to track him down. One is a hacker who specialized in obtaining contraband and the other works in a respected software company and (in my best Agent Smith impression)... helps his landlady take out her garbage.

Like Neo your offline security should get Top Billing, meaning the little pigtailed girl across the street should not think of you as 'that quiet, creepy dude who's cat Lucifer wails like a police siren at dinnertime' and keeps her up at night. They need to think positive thoughts.

They should trust you but not know *too* much. They only need to never suspect anything shady is going on - that you're good at fixing broken computers, bikes and love big dogs but you'd never do anything to hurt anyone. Never anything to do with any of the following: Tor. PGP. Freenet. I2P. Darkcoins. Especially Darkcoins or whatever flavor of the month they come in since they too change like the wind.

Pay cash for everything. Avoid social media outlets like the Black Plague. You know the ones. Facebook. Twitter. YouTube. Instagram. Pinterest. These are locales polluted with diseased gossip that'll turn any normal person into a zombie walker given enough time with an unrooted cell phone.

Neighbors gossip mainly about those they don't know. They fill in empty gaps with guesses and nonsense and sometimes outright lies. To prevent this, go to social engagements or pop in at backyard BBQs and be the one that has the best fireworks on the 4th of July, the same who bought expensive beer for everyone.

Be a volunteer at a shelter. A no-kill cat shelter. The Salvation Army. Help the neighborhood kids find their lost dog by going door to door with his pug mugshot you ripped off the telephone pole. Find him and they'll forgive you for accidentally launching a nuclear weapon in a Pentagon hack attempt.

You get busted, you'll want these people to speak up for you. Do all of the above and they'll form a standing army at your beck and call. Just never mention Tor, PGP and the rest, not even to dear old Dad who you can be quite certain will brag at every BBQ you go to that you're Snowden's long lost brother.

Change PGP keys frequently if and when your business grows. Avoid using any of your own handwriting on anything. Neither your name, address, favorite colors, nicknames you use on various forums.

Research the following:

Cashing Bitcoins
    Mail Anonymity/Stealth
    Stealth Materials
    Competitive Pricing
    Customer Service (i.e. How to keep your customers coming back for more).
    Sales copywriting. Read Cashvertising, a book on writing copy for anything.
    Research the best lawyer to have for whatever it is you're selling.

POSTAL DROPS & CONTROLLED DELIVERIES

Now for the real black market opsec. The first topic we'll discuss is controlled deliveries, a term used by those on both sides of the law.

What's a controlled delivery?

It's a way for law enforcement to dupe you into accepting a package containing illegal goods. It could be anything. Drugs. Guns. Japanese manga that involves underage 'cat' girls. All in the hopes you'll accept the package and make some off-the-cuff remark about the contents. They hope.

Then they can search your house. They need only establish you knew the package was coming, what it contained or what you intended on doing with it. Smoking it, of course, but one out of three is usually sufficient to get a search warrant. Let's dispense with a few myths first prior to counter-surveillance techniques.

<u>Myth #1: If a person receives any type of contraband in the mail, he can be arrested on the spot. Guilt by association</u>.

FALSE.

If receiving anything illegal in the mail is enough to send a guy to the Big House with Bubba, every school bully in existence could get sent up the creek by just ordering a few Scooby sheets of LSD to his house. It doesn't work that way. The police need proof that you know what's inside, otherwise it's a no-win case and they know it. If you're a cool level-headed, logical thinking kind of guy like Mr. Orange in Reservoir Dogs then they've got a problem. If they see your stone-cold blue eyes are filled with an Iron Man resolve, then they know their only recourse is to get you to flap your gums before the adrenaline 'fight or flight' rush wears off. To this end, there's a couple of effective ways they'd like to deal with you. Both involve deception.

The first is by taking the '**Nice Guy**' approach. You'd be shocked at how well they can get a stranger to spill his guts by playing up the nice guy angle. Be his friend so to speak. His father confessor.

When the heat is on and you've got a few stormtroopers stomping around your house with muddy boots, well, you want them to leave. I would too. And that's what they tell you. We'll leave, they'll say. Then the dirty tricks start. They make any newbie *want* to talk if only to relieve stress. Only he ends up spending *years* in prison instead of a measly three stinking days because he never kept his mouth shut.

Police officers and DEA agents in particular have had years to perfect the art of persuasion by deception. That means lying their ass off.

If you've ever seen Black Hawk Down then you know how ferocious a night raid can be, where they may have to 'clear' a house by going room to room and scaring the living hell out of anyone living there. It's scary stuff. The cat's smart enough to hide under the bed but Rover gets shot in the leg.

But it doesn't always go down that way.

You're usually seated in cuffs when the nice guy routine kicks into high gear. That's what they want to try first. Nice guy *then* mean guy and not the other way around since it's far easier to upgrade then to downgrade on the poor sap's emotions. Police usually say something like this.

"We only want the dealer, not you kid. Look, you're small time. We know it and you know it and your supplier knows it. You're useless to us. But your partner, your boss, he's the one we're after. The Big Fish. The Don. We see your family here and understand your situation, we've got our own. You're poor. You wanted to escape for an hour, maybe two. That's all. We understand. No trouble for you if you cooperate and tell us your source. Where'd you get these drugs from?"

You give Barney Fife a long silence as you fidget and glance around the room at where your hidden stash is. They'll say, "Talk so we can go home and you can get back to playing The Witcher on your laptop over there." (This is the part where they'll lie and say they're fans of the game themselves).

Should you talk?

Can they be trusted?

Then out of nowhere, when they see the synapses firing in your brain that tell you to keep your big trap shut, they bring out the 'Bad Guy' routine. Nice Guy's evil twin brother whose tone sounds an awful lot like the mouth of Sauron in the Lord of the Rings.

"Look kid, you're life's over. You're done. Cooked. You'll lose your kids in the next room over and your job and your car and your house and maybe even your cat sitting under the bed. She'll be put to sleep long before you get out of jail. Unless you just give us the name so we can cut you some slack, kid."

What's the first thing that's going to pop into your head if you're new to this?

- You want these clowns out of the house. Yesterday.
- You want a clean rep so the family doesn't think you're Jabba the Hutt.
- You want to believe them. They're dressed nice after all. Clean shaven. Shiny boots. Nice haircut. But then so was the Terminator when he went looking for Sarah Connor and her rebellious pain-in-the-ass son.

Bottom line: Don't fall for any of their lies. You see, when you're raided at some ungodly hour say at 6 AM, all the blood in your system goes to your legs and arms and you get what's called *brain drain*. You become a moron. A Ferengi or drunk Klingon say instead of a logical Vulcan who thinks clearly and invokes that God-given gift to all men called *discernment*. It's fight or flight time and the cops know most people won't use their brains at 6AM because they're used to seeing scrambled eggs. They'd rather fight, run away or just sign on the dotted line to shut em up so they'll leave, leave, LEAVE!

Don't let this happen. It's like walking right into Hell with both eyes wide open.

Don't talk to cops. Don't sign anything. Don't agree to anything.

Oh but you say you'd end up in jail? You'll end up there anyway regardless of what they tell you, only what they don't tell you is that 90% of the time, *if you keep your trap shut*, the prosecutor'll drop the case for insufficient evidence.

Most evidence comes from a confession, not from what the cops see or pick up on site.

Therefore never admit to a thing nor sign any 'apology' letter or anything else. Note that they'll try to get a confession before taking you down to the station. That's the whole point.

<u>Myth # 2: You Should Always Use a Fake Name or ID for a postal box.</u>

FALSE.

We briefly mentioned this one a few chapters ago, but it bears repeating. Whether you're using a UPS Store rental box or the post office, never ever use a fake ID or a false name. If one package of yours becomes compromised then you could be looking at a worse situation on account that they will know you lied. It'll look suspicious. Probable cause is much more likely a given if they know you're a liar. Be honest with non-law enforcement types. Honesty and silence work hand in hand but if you lied at some point along the way it'll be hard for you to deny any bad intentions with the rented box.

After 9/11 fake IDs get you into heaps of trouble these days, but doubly so for ordering darknet stuff. Now they're linked to everything from terrorism to identity theft to Silk Road-level drug empires. So in light of this, use your real name.

MYTH #3: Retrieve the package quick! Before anyone notices!

ALSO FALSE. You need to let it sit for a couple of days if at all possible. This is because the package is still 'hot'. Granted, police don't have unlimited funding that allows them to survey the store 24/7/365 days a year, even for a small fish who needs a break. But if any bust is going down it'll likely happen fast.

From there you can take it to a neutral spot and open it somewhere safe. Or you could wait a few days later to add that extra layer of plausible deniability about the contents of the package. Again this goes back to our opsec mindset and living out that opsec mindset day to day, hour to hour, by taking action beforehand. That is, having a clear plan ahead of time as well as a Plan B, a Plan C, etc.

ESCAPING THE WEST!

Disclaimer: Note that it's now a serious felony (at least in the U.S.) to resort to this method. 9/11 changed everything. Your mileage may vary.

The gauntlet's been thrown down. The challenge issued. You've got about six months to cash in a few assets to get your money and your sorry-you-ever-married-a-Toronto-girl hide out of Dodge for good or else a court judgment will fly down like a bolt of lightning from Zeus to your arse that'll leave you wailing like those alley cats on Bourbon Street.

You've been over it a thousand times. If you don't hightail it you just know a police cruiser will be along at any moment to arrest you for whistling a copyrighted tune out your backside - and then you'll be seeing red-blue flashbacks with every trip to the john.

Six months. Six months. What's a decent guy to do? How do you start a brand new life abroad with only a U.S. passport and less than a hundred grand to your name? Where do you go and how do you prevent a tail? Is the IRS's long reach an urban myth? Student loans? Child support for that illegal you shagged in Phoenix?

Extradition laws vary but you've little desire to learn Thai or Vietnamese and zero will to fight off the Zeta cartel's pack of little league brigade in Monterray. You need an escape plan.

Let's assume you've no qualms about breaking any further laws at this point. Being thrown beyond the pearly gates, there's little reason to keep playing that rusty old harp so you'll break a few laws on the way down hoping no one Really Big will take notice.

The first thing you must do is change your identity. There's a few ways to go about it. The simplest way is to steal someone else's. Someone who won't care. Someone who, frankly, isn't here anymore. A baby. Yep that's right, a baby whose gone up to the pearly gates but on the way up managed to drop that shiny new social security number when his wings popped out.

Thousands of babies never make it past a year in this world of rain and failure. They pass on, greener pastures and all that, God Bless em, but the names of those tykes are still in the system. Your system. The same one you've been paying your hard-earned money into for all your life. So you need to research deceased citizens who died when they were young, preferably around your age. This is the one time in all of human existence when Google is really your friend.

You get the number and that's the number you'll use for a new driver's license, passport, bank account or even credit union. Combine that with and off-shore holding corp and you may have a winning combination.

It may be that the deceased is in fact listed in the Social

Security Administration's system as 'deceased'. Not always, but sometimes. Your mission is to keep trying until you get one that isn't in this beast of a system. Getting a new number isn't easy peasy. The brigands that run that maniacal ship often require an in-person interview before they give it. Again, not always, and it'd be quite embarrassing to explain how you got by the last 30 years without one or a driver's license.

But if the illegals can do it, so can you IF you've got nothing to lose. Nothing is set in stone where the government is concerned and for the record they catch more rule-followers than rule-breakers.

That said, read again the disclaimer at the top of this chapter. Sneaking into Canada (even if you're Canadian citizen) without stopping into the checkpoint is also a felony, one that's punishable by a $5000 dollar fine.

Sniffer Dogs & Cash

When going through customs checkpoints, keep in mind that there are dogs that are trained to sniff out money. Some dogs are gifted that way. Some of them can even sniff out cancer. People not living near the border think these dogs are out all the damn time. It isn't true. I live in Canada and can tell you I've seen a dog twice, both times on sunny bright flower days and happy as a clam. But on a rainy day? Here's a little police secret: cops hate working in the rain just as much as sniffer dogs.

State troopers in particular would rather sit in their police cruiser and wait till the rain stops on the interstate from say, New Orleans to Phoenix, to resume ticket writing or searches. That's why if you're a smuggler or just a guy who likes to bring a little reefer along on a long beach trip, you leave on a rainy day. Same with customs. On some days, the rain and snow fly in *sideways*.

Now then. Back to the sniffer dogs. Snoopy can separate scents so hiding cash or drugs in mustard isn't going to work. His big wet nose can smell weed even under your nails to say nothing about clothes. Most of these dogs though are trained to sniff out the serious drugs, drugs like heroin, MDMA, cocaine and every other drug imaginable. And cash. Oh yes. Cash has quite a strong scent. Take out a couple grand from your bank account and when you get it home, take a long whiff of it. It's potent stuff and I read one account that said there's traces of cocaine on every $100 dollar bill in the US.

A sealed ziploc bag will get you through 50% of the time though, provided the bag is washed thoroughly and any residue on the outside has been rinsed away. The problem here is that weed, like cash, gives off a very potent odor and given enough time the scent will permeate through the plastic. So you must do this within hours of travel. The longer it's in there the more risky it gets that the smell has permeated through the seal to reach the dog's wet nose.

One thing to remember though, is that the primary function of a sniffer dog is to act as a **legal prop**, regardless of what you're carrying.

Let's say you get profiled. You're a twenty-something, college aged, black-skinned, black-haired tattooed-up probable drug user. You get pulled over on some pretense to secondary inspection coming into Canada. You refuse consent to any search. The cop brings a drug dog and that dog <u>ALERTS</u> (according to the cop) like you've got Cheech and Chong hidden in the trunk with 100 pounds of coke. Now the cop has a probable cause for a warrantless search.

"The dog barked so he must be a terrorist!" (though they don't generally alert by barking).

Regardless, it's almost always the officer who targets you in 95% of the cases and it almost never matters whether the dog can smell anything or not, just that the dog was present and the cop "testifies" that it alerted. This is true with cash, drugs or the preggo alien in the back seat from Men in Black. Doesn't matter what it is.

Also, you don't legally have to wait for them to bring the drug dog because doing so would constitute a detainment - which they cannot do unless they are arresting you on specific grounds. If they threaten you with it you should ask if you're being detained. When they inevitably say "no," that's your cue to LEAVE. Just make sure that any other issues (like a speeding ticket) are already taken care of so that the cop doesn't go back to his/her car and just sit on your driver's license until the dog shows up.

Sailboats

Sailboats can be an effective way to disappear, with a few caveats. Do you hold a US passport? If you do then why do you need someone's permission to leave the coast? Hire a skipper you trust (and a first mate!) if you can't sail and just need to get from point A to point B. Blue water boats you can buy on the cheap (relatively speaking) for about 20 grand. You'd want to go someplace with a less than reliable immigration control system, obviously. A place without an extradition treaty with the U.S.

Laos perhaps? It's your port of call but sailing around southwest Asia is about as low-key as a guy can get without kicking off a new career as a Tibetan monk. The downside is that you can get a little too comfortable in other places like the Mediterranean and end up exposing your new identity to first world officials and their beast systems. You don't want to end up in someplace that's quickly turning into a shadow of the USA.

Are you broke? Don't sweat it. It's mostly a mental barrier which, if you get to a safe harbor somewhere abroad, you'll see it never was a barrier at all. If you lack cold hard cash and need to flee with little in the way of records being assigned to your hot name, lots of boats lack enough crewmen to do the job. They've got their own safety to worry about. If they not enough men, they don't sail. They'll take you in if you ask with a smile.

'Hop aboard!' they'll say after you've promised to pay for the cheap beer. You can forget about getting paid like the rest, though they'll probably throw you some scraps. That's good enough. The real hurdle is to hop on a boat that won't create a paper trail (as in no centralized system). Somewhere that doesn't assign you a number to track you to your dying breath. A place like Cambodia now that I think about it. If you've ever seen Cambodian border checkpoints then you know how lax they can be.

Either way, be sure to record your adventure on camera: Boarding a ship, working as a crew member, adventure unknown.

Thank you for reading. Book 2 is available for purchase now

Or read on for a sneak peek of The Invisibility Toolkit below!

∼

Winston Churchill once said, "If you find yourself in Hell... keep going."

I can relate to that as easily as you can. But these days Hell itself seems to have taken on an altogether foreign form that's wholly different than the medieval version. These days, many 'angels of light' profess to know what's good for us better than we do ourselves - which is sheer lunacy.

We're not sheep. We all see it. We're not blind. And some of us want to act as beacons of light in a sea of darkness rather than go "Baaaaa!" like sheep to the bloody slaughter. We want to lead others away from the slaughterhouse. But to do that requires a specific set of skills that you don't learn in college.

Skills that will help us turn back the tide of Armageddon on individual sovereignty. Because let's face it, attacks on privacy have increased a thousand-fold. Every day new laws are passed that make privacy as rare as pink diamonds. In the future privacy may become as valuable as pink diamonds. Do you want to hear your grandkids ask you what it was like in the old days when people were *not* monitored 24/7?

Right. Didn't think so.

It's high-time we fought back and fought hard. If you've ever seen the Shawshank Redemption then you know what happens to weaklings - those that don't take action. They get raped again and again and again. Sooner or later you'll know the meaning of this phrase: "His judgment cometh and that right soon." It means war. Wouldn't you rather fight before the raping and pillaging starts? I would.

Judgment Day is already here. You cannot walk down the street without meeting a dozen street cams, and as an American-Canadian citizen there are times when I've wanted to disappear from society altogether. Vanish as though I'd slipped Frodo's elvish cloak over my neck and smoothed that runic ring right down my middle finger before flipping off the elites in power.

But first, a little story.

A story way back in 2001.

Living in close proximity to the housing projects of New Orleans, most days driving back from the University of New Orleans were uneventful. For the most part. Only Mardi Gras seemed to break the monotony along with eating soggy beignets (powdered donuts) on Bourbon Street.

Except for one day in particular while sweating in Manila-like traffic. On that day something terrifying happened. I decided to take a shortcut which turned out to be a shortcut into trouble. Before I knew it, a fourteen-year-old girl, black with ripped jeans, red sweatshirt and a nose that could put a bloodhound to shame ran in front of my beat-up Camaro while I drove 15MPH.

I slammed on the brakes and missed her hip by an inch. She slammed her fists on the hood of my car. Boom. Then she flipped me off real casual like this sort of thing happened every time it rained. I hopped out, furious, and proceeded to make sure she knew how close she'd come to a date with the grim reaper.

A cacophony of yelling ensued with every color of the rainbows. Soft swearing, hard swearing, and sweating (mostly me) as she matched every curse word with one better, more deviant, and fueled with twice the rage as though she'd been bred for no other reason than to unleash it all on me on that fiery summer day. A vampiric Lady Macbeth, this thug was. But none of that really mattered to the law. No sir, what mattered was when I grabbed her arm and stabbed a finger into her face as I shouted to be more careful. I began to walk away.

Only I wasn't going anywhere.

Her brother came running. A BIG brother wearing a dozen gold chains and carrying a chain big enough to tie a velociraptor. I swear the guy looked straight out of the A-Team. After that, her mother came screaming and what I presumed at the time was her grandmother, broom in hand (a witch?). I panicked as the big brother threw me to the ground as mama called the cops. I remember expecting a black cat to come along any minute to scratch my face to shreds. I was going down in flames though I was innocent of any abuse.

Fast-forward three weeks later and I'm having my ass handed to me by the most militant judge I'd ever laid eyes on. A real man hater whose harpy-like claws seemed to grow the more I sweat. I had only one choice: Play along. So I kissed ass like I'd never done before in my whole miserable life. At the end of her screeching rant, I ended up getting off on a technicality. The police had screwed up somewhere, it seemed.

My record was as clean as a babe's arse. Clear as crystal.

Or so I thought. Later that year, a detective came knocking. It seemed that the little girl had disappeared, and to my horror it turned out that he knew everything about *me*. Things that were not in the court transcript. Things I'd done were recorded by various cameras set up around the city. The entire city seemed to be turning a shade Orwellian.

"Talk to me," he said smiling with that shiny badge gleaming. I frowned. Talk to the cops? "Yeah," he replied. "Talk to me or get put on the sex offender's list for abusing that little girl."

Abuse?

I clammed up. Granted, I was naive, but not stupid. He ended up letting me go after throwing down every threat imaginable. After that I wanted to vanish even more, and as I would later learn, I wasn't the first to go through such an ordeal.

Up until that point, I'd always trusted the police, or for that matter any kind of higher authority in government. I trusted the media. I trusted newspapers. I trusted juries. About the only thing I never trusted were the palm readers who always set up shop around the French Quarter.

Well, no longer.

From that point on, I swore to myself I'd learn how to be invisible, or die trying. True, I escaped the sex offender registry by keeping my mouth shut. Others have not been so lucky. I've heard another author (Wendy McElroy) relate a similar story:

"Last summer, an Illinois man lost an appeal on his conviction as a sex offender for grabbing the arm of a 14-year-old girl. She had stepped directly in front of his car, causing him to swerve in order to avoid hitting her.

Fitzroy Barnaby was 28 years old. He jumped out his car, grabbed her arm and lectured her on how not to get killed. Nothing more occurred. Nevertheless, that one action made him guilty of "the unlawful restraint of a minor," which is a sexual offense in Illinois. Both the jury and the judge believed him. Nevertheless, Barnaby went through years of legal proceedings that ended with his name on a sex offender registry, where his photograph and address were publicly available. He must report to authorities. His employment options are severely limited; he cannot live near schools or parks."

Here I was thinking I was the only guy that had experienced such a horrific day. The absurd part is not even that it happened. It's that it is never forgiven. It's never put in the past where mistakes are buried. They are broadcast forever, branded over and over into our memories. Forgiveness, that is, granting your past actions invisible to everyone but you and the Almighty, is outlawed.

Well. This book aims to reverse that trend. It aims to give you back your privacy and if you need it, **invisibility**.

You don't want newspaper reporters sticking mics in your face before you've had your day in court do you? This happened to me. I remember feeling like I'd killed everyone's favorite rock star.

Think on how your life would change if this happened to you:

- Someone uses your unsecured WiFi to threaten the President.
- A hacker steals your credit card to buy Russian child porn using proxies.
- You hear sirens just as your phone rings. You pick up to hear a TV reporter asking for an interview since you were the last person to see the Governor alive at the Beau Chene Country Club - who was later found dead in a pool of blood in the restroom - the same one you used.
- The powers that be are coming after you for child support - without allowing you to see your own children. You try to visit Canada to "get away from it all" for a while, when you are *arrested* at the border. Things get worse when they find a few "manga" comics in your back seat. Manga that is illegal in Canada but not the USA. Chaos ensues. They rip your reputation apart in the name of *the law*.
- Your ten year old brother jokes to his pals on the school yard that he has a shed full of Rambo-like grenades and a few barrels of gunpowder. A girl overhears. She snitches. The cop arrest *him* (not kidding) but later let him go. Years later, that report shows up when he tries to join the Marines. He is *rejected*. Yes, this really happened to a relative in Louisiana. And that's not to say Louisiana is any better or

worse than any other state where hysteria can run amok and drag you along for the ride. The fact is, I'll show you how to prevent crap like this from happening no matter which country you are in.

If you are ever investigated, the authorities will likely tear your place apart looking for anything to build a solid case to hand to the prosecutor. Who knows what your situation might be at that time. You might need to go away for a while to strategize with attorneys, maintain your business, speak to family, move assets, etc. It is difficult to do that from a jail cell.

The USA now has a "guilty until proven innocent" legal system. You are not innocent until proven guilty, but I will teach you how to gain that precious commodity called TIME which you can use to gather resources to defend yourself. Resources that go well with becoming **invisible**.

You will learn:

1.) How to be anonymous *offline* as well as on.

2.) How to use your surroundings to lessen risk, special forces style.

3.) How to detect when you are being data-mined: How to hide where you went to school, where you've lived, whom you've loved, whom you did not. Your shopping habits, dating habits, political affiliations. You get the picture.

4.) How to look like a small fish and not a BIG FISH. And that's just the beginning.